Guard Your Money

The Simple YubiKey Guide for Financial Security

L. Phillips

PRAIRIE LIGHT PRESS
ESTD. 2025

Helping readers move from the unknown to the known

Published by Prairie Light Press

Second Edition

English Edition

Publication Identifiers:

ISBN (Hardcover) 9798996980253
ISBN (Paperback) 979-8278628415
ASIN (Kindle) B0G6VG38X1

This book is provided for informational and educational purposes only.

Disclaimer

The information contained in this book is provided for educational purposes only.

The author makes no representations or warranties regarding the accuracy, completeness, or suitability of the information contained herein. The techniques and procedures described may not be appropriate for all systems or environments.

The author shall not be held liable for any loss, damage, or disruption caused by reliance on the information provided in this book.

Readers are responsible for evaluating and applying the information in accordance with their own circumstances and applicable laws.

No Affiliation Statement

Any product names, logos, brands, or trademarks referenced in this book are the property of their respective owners, YubiCo, and YubiKey.. Their use does not imply endorsement.

Table of Contents

Introduction: Why Your Money Isn't Safe (And How to Fix It)

Let me ask you something: How much money do you have in your bank account right now? Your investment accounts? Your retirement savings?

Now imagine waking up tomorrow morning, checking your phone, and seeing that it's all gone. Every penny. Transferred to someone you've never met, in a country you've never visited.

Sound like a nightmare? It happened to Sarah, a 52-year-old teacher from Ohio. She thought she was logging into her bank's website—it looked identical to the real thing. She entered her username and password like she'd done a thousand times before. Within 30 minutes, $43,000 was gone from her savings account.

Or how about Tom, a retired veteran who had his entire retirement account at Schwab drained after someone intercepted a text message code sent to his phone. The thieves used something called 'SIM swapping' to take over his phone number, and the bank's text message security didn't stand a chance.

These aren't rare cases. In 2024 alone, Americans lost over $12.5 billion to online fraud and cybercrime. That's billion with a 'B.' And it's getting worse every single day.

The Problem Is Simple

Your passwords aren't enough anymore. Even if you use a different password for every account (and let's be honest, most people don't), hackers have gotten incredibly sophisticated. They can:

- Send you emails that look EXACTLY like they're from your bank
- Create fake websites that are pixel-perfect copies of the real thing
- Intercept the 'security codes' sent to your phone via text message
- Install invisible malware on your computer that records everything you type
- Hijack your phone number so THEY receive your security codes

The scariest part? You can do everything right—use strong passwords, be careful about emails, keep your software updated—and STILL get hacked. Because the system itself is broken.

But There's a Solution

This book is about one simple device that changes everything: the YubiKey.

Think of a YubiKey like a physical key for your online accounts. It's a small device, about the size of your car key fob, that you plug into your computer or tap on your phone. Without it, nobody—and I mean NOBODY—can access your money, even if they have your password.

- Not the hacker in Russia who phished your password.
- Not the scammer who cloned your phone.
- Not even the sophisticated criminal who installed malware on your laptop.

If they don't have your physical YubiKey in their hands, they can't get to your money. Period.

Who This Book Is For

This book is for regular people who want to protect their money without becoming computer experts. You don't need to understand encryption algorithms or cryptographic protocols. You just need to follow simple, step-by-step instructions.

If you:

- Have money in a bank account, investment account, or retirement fund
- Want to sleep better at night knowing your finances are protected
- Are tired of worrying about getting hacked or scammed
- Don't want to become a tech expert just to stay safe

...then this book is for you.

What You'll Learn

By the end of this book, you'll know exactly how to:

- Buy the right YubiKey for your needs (they're surprisingly affordable)
- Set it up with your bank, investment accounts, email, and password manager
- Create a backup YubiKey and store it safely (this is crucial!)
- Use your YubiKey every day without any hassle
- Protect your entire family's financial accounts

- Recover if something goes wrong

I'll give you specific, step-by-step instructions for the major financial institutions: Chase, Bank of America, Wells Fargo, Vanguard, Fidelity, Schwab, and JPMorgan Chase. No technical jargon. No confusing terms. Just simple, clear directions that anyone can follow.

A Small Investment for Huge Peace of Mind

A YubiKey costs between $25 and $70 depending on the model. That's it. One-time purchase. No monthly fees. No subscriptions.

Compare that to the billions of dollars lost to cybercrime every year, and it's the easiest decision you'll ever make.

So let's get started. Your money is waiting to be protected, and it's easier than you think.

Turn the page, and let's make your financial accounts virtually unhackable.

Chapter 1: Understanding the Threats

Before we talk about the solution, you need to understand what you're up against. And I promise you, it's scarier than you think—but also more preventable than you might imagine.

Phishing: The Wolf in Sheep's Clothing

You've probably heard the term 'phishing' before. But let me show you how sophisticated it's become.

Here's what happened to Jennifer, a marketing director in Seattle:

- She received an email that appeared to be from Chase Bank. The logo was perfect. The formatting was identical. The email address looked legitimate: 'security@chase-alerts.com'. The message said there was suspicious activity on her account and she needed to verify her identity immediately.

- She clicked the link. The website looked EXACTLY like Chase's real website. She entered her username and password. Within seconds, the real criminals had her credentials and were logging into her actual account.

- The kicker? The fake website even showed her real account balance (they grabbed it in real-time after she logged in), so she had no idea anything was wrong. By the time she realized what happened, $18,000 had been wire transferred out of her account.

⚠ **WARNING: Modern phishing emails are nearly impossible to detect by eye. Even security professionals get fooled.**

Malware: The Silent Thief

Malware is malicious software that gets installed on your computer without you knowing. It can:

- Record every keystroke you type (including passwords)
- Take screenshots of your banking sessions
- Modify websites you visit to steal your information
- Run completely invisibly in the background for months

How does it get on your computer? Sometimes from shady websites, but often from sources you trust:

- Fake software updates that look legitimate
- Email attachments from addresses that appear to be from friends
- Infected USB drives
- Even compromised legitimate websites you visit regularly

SIM Swapping: When Your Phone Number Betrays You

This one is particularly nasty because it exploits a security measure that's supposed to PROTECT you: text message verification codes.

Here's how it works:

- A scammer calls your cell phone carrier pretending to be you
- They claim they 'lost' their phone and need to transfer your number to a new SIM card
- They provide just enough personal information (often gathered from social media or data breaches) to convince the carrier they're really you

- The carrier transfers your phone number to a SIM card that the criminal controls
- Now when your bank sends a 'security code' via text message, the criminal receives it—not you
- They drain your accounts while you're left wondering why your phone suddenly stopped working

This happened to Michael Terpin, a cryptocurrency investor, who lost $24 million in a single SIM swap attack. But it's not just happening to rich people—everyday Americans lose thousands of dollars to this scam every single day.

Password Database Breaches

Even if YOU do everything right with your passwords, the companies you trust might not.

- Major data breaches in recent years:
- Yahoo: 3 billion accounts
- LinkedIn: 700 million accounts
- Adobe: 153 million accounts
- Home Depot: 56 million payment cards

When these breaches happen, criminals get access to usernames, passwords, email addresses, and sometimes even credit card information. Then they try those same credentials on OTHER websites, betting (correctly) that most people reuse passwords.

If you used the same password for LinkedIn that you use for your bank? They're in.

The Shocking Statistics

Let's talk numbers, because they're staggering:

- 81% of data breaches are caused by weak, reused, or stolen passwords (Verizon, 2024)
- Americans lost $12.5 billion to cybercrime in 2024
- The average cost of a data breach for a company: $4.45 million
- 95% of cybersecurity breaches are caused by human error
- A new phishing website is created every 20 seconds

And here's the stat that should really wake you up: The FBI reports that people over 60 lost $3.4 billion to internet scams in 2023 alone. Criminals specifically target older Americans because they tend to have more savings and may be less familiar with online security.

Why Traditional Security Doesn't Work Anymore

'Strong passwords' aren't enough. Even if you create a password like 'Xk#9mP$2qL@7vN!5' and never write it down, it can still be:

- Phished (you type it into a fake website)
- Keystroke-logged by malware
- Stolen in a database breach
- Intercepted if the website doesn't use proper encryption

'Security questions' are a joke. What was your first pet's name? Your mother's maiden name? The street you grew up on? This information is often publicly available on social media or can be easily guessed.

'Text message codes' can be intercepted through SIM swapping, as we discussed. They're better than nothing, but they're not secure enough for your money.

'Authenticator apps' (like Google Authenticator) are better than text messages, but they can still be compromised if your phone is stolen or hacked.

So What DOES Work?

Physical security keys like the YubiKey.

Here's why they're virtually unhackable:

- Phishing doesn't work – Even if you enter your password on a fake website, the scammer can't use it without your physical key
- Malware doesn't work – Recording your keystrokes is useless if they also need the physical device in your pocket
- SIM swapping doesn't work – Your phone number is irrelevant when you're using a hardware key
- Database breaches don't matter – Even if a company's password database is stolen, attackers still can't access your account without your key

Think of it this way: A burglar might pick your door lock, but they can't pick a lock that doesn't exist. With a YubiKey, there IS no lock for them to pick remotely. They would need to physically steal the device from you—and even then, they'd still need your password.

💡 **TIP: Security experts and major corporations use hardware keys for a reason. Google has been using them internally since 2017 and reports ZERO successful phishing attacks against employees who use them.**

In the next chapter, we'll talk about exactly what a YubiKey is and how it works. And don't worry—it's way simpler than you think.

Chapter 2: What Is a YubiKey? (In Plain English)

Alright, let's demystify this thing. If you've never heard of a YubiKey before, or if you have but you're not quite sure what it does, this chapter will make everything crystal clear.

The Car Key Analogy

- Think about your car key. Even if someone knows:
- Your car's make and model

- Where you park it
- Your license plate number
- That you always keep the owner's manual in the glove box

...they STILL can't drive your car without the physical key, right?

- A YubiKey works the same way for your online accounts. Even if hackers know:
- Your username
- Your password
- Your email address
- Your phone number

...they STILL can't access your account without the physical YubiKey that's in your pocket (or wherever you keep it safe).

What Does It Look Like?

Figure 1. YubiKey 5 NFC on a keyring. Photograph © 2026 L. Phillips/Prairie Light Press

A YubiKey is a small device, roughly the size of your car key fob or a USB flash drive. Most models are about 1.5 inches long and less than an inch wide. It's durable (you can literally put it through the washing machine and it'll still work), waterproof, and has no battery to charge.

The most common model has:

- A USB connector (either USB-A or USB-C, just like a regular USB stick)
- A gold circle or square on the flat surface (this is what you touch to activate it)
- Optional NFC capability (for tapping on your phone)

There are no buttons to press, no screens to read, and nothing complicated about it. It's literally just a small piece of hardware that you plug in or tap when asked.

How It's Different From Text Message Codes

You might be thinking, 'But my bank already sends me security codes via text message. Isn't that good enough?'

Short answer: No. Here's why:

When your bank sends you a code via text message, that code is:

- Traveling through the air (can be intercepted)
- Stored on your phone (can be accessed if your phone is hacked)
- Tied to your phone number (can be redirected via SIM swapping)
- Vulnerable to social engineering attacks on your carrier

With a YubiKey:

- Nothing travels through the air—the authentication happens directly between the key and the website

- Nothing is stored anywhere—each authentication generates a unique, one-time cryptographic signature
- Your phone number is irrelevant—the key doesn't use it
- Nobody can call your carrier and trick them—there's no carrier involved

💡 TIP: The National Institute of Standards and Technology (NIST) recommends deprecating SMS-based authentication due to security vulnerabilities. Hardware keys like YubiKey are their recommended alternative.

The Science Made Simple (No Geek Speak, I Promise)

Okay, I know you didn't buy this book for a computer science lesson, but understanding the basics helps you trust the system. I'll keep this REALLY simple.

When you set up a YubiKey with, say, your bank:

- The YubiKey and the bank exchange mathematical 'handshakes' (called cryptographic keys)
- These handshakes are unique to YOUR YubiKey and YOUR bank account

- Every time you log in, your YubiKey proves it's the same device without revealing any secret information
- Even if hackers intercept the communication, they can't copy or reuse it

It's like having a secret handshake with your bank that changes every single time and can't be faked. Nobody else knows the handshake, and even if they watch you do it, they can't recreate it.

The beautiful part? You don't have to understand how it works. You just plug it in (or tap it), touch the gold circle, and you're authenticated. That's it.

Why Hackers Can't Fake It

Here's the crucial part: Unlike a password (which is just information that can be copied), a YubiKey uses physical hardware that generates unique cryptographic signatures.

To fake a YubiKey, a hacker would need to:

- Steal or copy the mathematical secrets stored in the hardware (essentially impossible without physical access and specialized equipment)

- Break the cryptographic algorithms (would take longer than the age of the universe with current computers)
- Somehow predict the unique signature it will generate next (mathematically impossible)

Even nation-state actors with unlimited resources can't break this. That's why the U.S. government, major tech companies, and high-security organizations all use hardware security keys.

Which YubiKey Should You Buy?

Yubico (the company that makes YubiKeys) offers several models. Don't let the choices overwhelm you—I'll break it down simply.

The YubiKey 5 NFC – Best for Most People ($45)

This is the model I recommend for almost everyone. Here's why:

- Works with computers (USB-A port, found on most computers)
- Works with phones (NFC means you can tap it on your iPhone or Android)
- Compatible with virtually every service that supports security keys

- Durable and waterproof
- No battery needed—it powers itself from the USB port

The YubiKey 5C NFC – For Newer Laptops ($55)

If your computer only has USB-C ports (the newer, smaller reversible port), get this model instead. It has all the same features as the 5 NFC, just with a USB-C connector.

The YubiKey 5Ci – For Apple Users ($70)

This one has both USB-C AND a Lightning connector, making it perfect for people with iPhones and iPads. It's the most versatile but also the most expensive.

The Security Key Series – Budget Option ($25-30)

If budget is tight, Yubico also makes a 'Security Key' series that's more affordable. These work great for basic protection but have fewer advanced features. For protecting your bank accounts, they're perfectly adequate.

💡 TIP: Not sure which USB port you have? Look at your computer's USB ports. USB-A is the rectangular port you've been using for years. USB-C is newer, smaller, and oval-shaped. Most computers have at least one USB-A port, but newer laptops might only have USB-C.

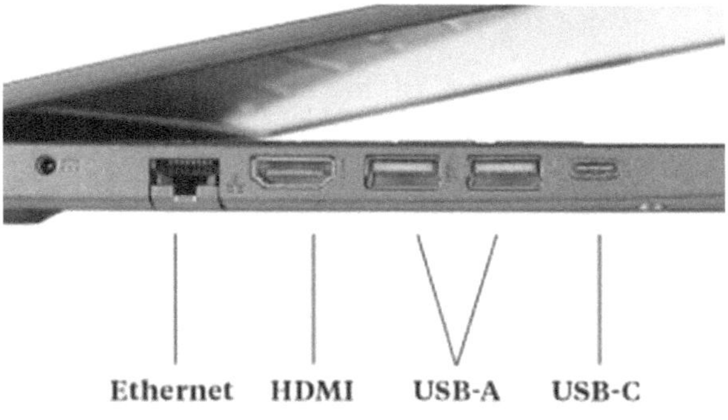

How Much Do They Cost?

Here's the straight pricing (as of 2025):

- Security Key Series: $25-30
- YubiKey 5 NFC: $45
- YubiKey 5C NFC: $55
- YubiKey 5Ci: $70

Remember, this is a ONE-TIME purchase. No subscriptions, no monthly fees, no annual renewals. You buy it once, and it lasts for years.

And here's my recommendation: Buy TWO. Yes, two. One for daily use, and one as a backup that you'll store somewhere safe (more on this in Chapter 6). So budget for roughly $100-$140 depending on which model you choose.

I know that might seem like a lot, but compare it to:

- The $18,000 Jennifer lost to a phishing attack
- The $43,000 Sarah lost when her password was compromised
- The peace of mind knowing your life savings are protected

It's the cheapest insurance you'll ever buy.

Do You Really Need Two Keys?

Yes. Absolutely. 100% yes.

Here's why: If you only have one YubiKey and you lose it, you'll be locked out of all your accounts until you can go through lengthy recovery processes with each service. Some services make recovery difficult (on purpose, for security), and you might be locked out for days or even weeks.

With a backup key that's registered to all the same accounts:

- You can access your accounts immediately if you lose your primary key
- You can keep the backup in a safe place (home safe, safety deposit box, trusted family member's house)
- You have peace of mind knowing you won't get locked out

Think of it like having a spare car key. You hope you never need it, but you're REALLY glad you have it when you lock your keys in the car.

In the next chapter, we'll walk through actually buying your YubiKeys and making sure you get authentic ones (yes, counterfeits exist, unfortunately).

Chapter 3: Getting Started: Your First YubiKey

Alright, decision time. You know what a YubiKey is, why you need one, and which model to get. Now let's actually buy it and make sure you're getting the real deal.

Where to Buy Authentic YubiKeys

This is important because, yes, counterfeit YubiKeys exist. You want to make absolutely sure you're buying from a legitimate source.

Official Yubico Website (Recommended)

The safest place to buy is directly from yubico.com. You're guaranteed to get an authentic product, and they often run promotions or bundle deals.

Pros: 100% authentic, latest models, official warranty, customer support

Cons: Shipping takes a few days, sometimes slightly more expensive

Amazon

Amazon sells YubiKeys, but make sure you're buying from 'Yubico' as the seller, not a third-party seller.

⚠ WARNING: Only buy from Amazon if it says 'Ships from and sold by Amazon.com' or 'Ships from and sold by Yubico'. Avoid third-party sellers, as counterfeits have been found.

Authorized Retailers

Yubico has authorized retailers including Best Buy and some enterprise IT suppliers. Check yubico.com/store-locator for a list of authorized retailers in your area.

What to Look for When It Arrives

When your YubiKey arrives, check these things to make sure it's authentic:

- Official Packaging: Should come in sealed Yubico packaging with clear branding

- Quality: The device should feel solid and well-made, not flimsy or cheap
- Serial Number: Each YubiKey has a unique serial number printed on it
- Works Immediately: Real YubiKeys work right out of the box, no software installation needed

💡 **TIP: Yubico has a guide on their website showing what authentic packaging looks like. Visit yubico.com/authentication-standards/how-to-verify-authenticity to check yours.**

Unboxing Your YubiKey

When you open the package, you'll find:

- The YubiKey iself
- A quick start guide (usually just a card with basic info)
- That's it!

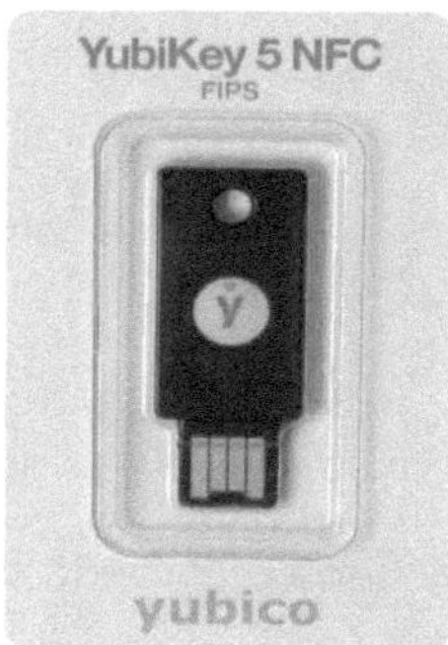

There's no software CD, no instruction manual, no complicated setup wizard. The YubiKey is designed to just work. You'll set it up with each individual service (your bank, email, etc.), which we'll cover in the next chapter.

Testing Your New YubiKey

Before you register it with any important accounts, let's make sure it works. Here's a simple test:

1. Go to demo.yubico.com on your computer
2. Plug your YubiKey into a USB port
3. Click in the text field on the demo page
4. Touch the gold circle on your YubiKey
5. You should see a long string of random characters appear

If that worked, congratulations! Your YubiKey is functioning properly. That string of characters is called a One-Time Password (OTP), and it's one of the ways YubiKeys can authenticate you.

Understanding the Different Ports

Let's make sure you know how to use your YubiKey with different devices:

For Computers (USB Connection)

- USB-A keys: Plug into the rectangular USB port on your computer
- USB-C keys: Plug into the smaller, oval USB-C port
- Adapter: If you have a USB-A key but only USB-C ports (or vice versa), you can buy a simple adapter for a few dollars

For Phones (NFC Connection)

iPhone: Hold the YubiKey against the back of your phone (where the camera is) and wait for a prompt

Android: Tap the YubiKey on the back of your phone, usually near the center

Note: NFC only works if you have a model with NFC capability (like the YubiKey 5 NFC or 5C NFC). Check your model number if you're unsure.

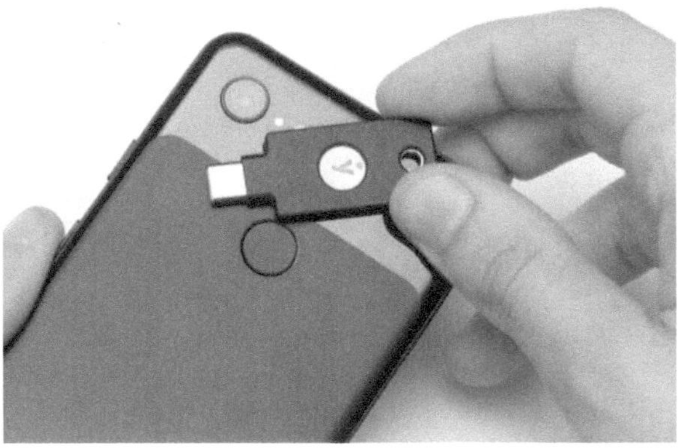

Important: Buy Your Backup Key Now

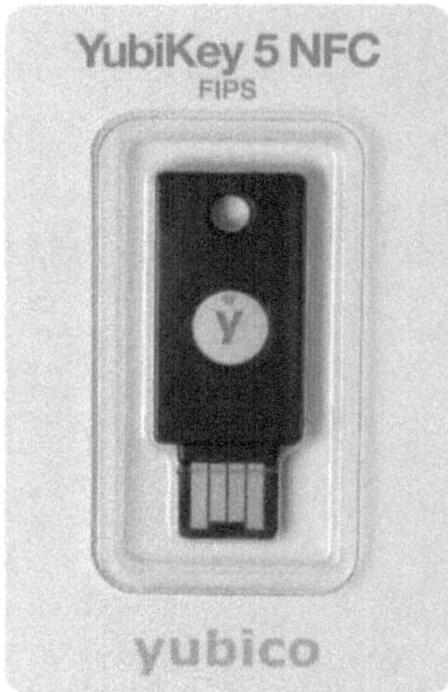

I'm going to say this again because it's crucial: Order your backup key RIGHT NOW. Don't wait. Don't think 'I'll get it later.' Get it now while you're thinking about it.

Why?

You want to register both keys at the same time with each service (way easier than doing it twice)

If you wait and then lose your primary key, you're stuck

You'll forget if you don't do it now

You don't need an identical model for your backup. For example, if you bought a YubiKey 5 NFC for daily use, your backup could be the cheaper Security Key model. They'll both work the same way with your accounts.

Labeling Your Keys (Smart Idea)

Once you have both keys, label them so you don't get confused:

- Use a label maker or a piece of tape and a permanent marker
- Write 'PRIMARY' on one and 'BACKUP' on the other
- Or use colored labels/tags to differentiate them

This seems obvious now, but trust me—six months from now when you have two identical-looking keys, you'll be glad you labeled them.

💡 **TIP: Some people use colored key covers or silicone sleeves for their YubiKeys. These not only protect the key but also make it easy to tell your primary and backup apart.**

Where to Keep Your Primary Key

Your primary YubiKey should be accessible but safe. Good options:

- On your regular keychain (attached with a key ring)
- In your wallet or purse (if it doesn't add too much bulk)
- In a desk drawer if you primarily work from home
- On a lanyard around your neck (if you're comfortable with that)

The key is to have it with you when you need it but not somewhere you're likely to lose it. Treat it like your house keys—something you check for before leaving home.

We'll talk about where to keep your backup key in Chapter 6, but for now, just keep it somewhere safe at home until you've set up both keys with your accounts.

In the next chapter, we're going to dive into actually setting up your YubiKey with your most important accounts. This is where the magic happens.

Chapter 4: Setting Up Your YubiKey (Step-by-Step)

This is where the magic begins. In this chapter, we're going to walk through setting up your YubiKey with the most important accounts you have — your bank, your investment accounts, and your primary email.

Because here's the truth:

Your YubiKey is only as strong as the accounts you connect it to.

So in this chapter, you'll get:

- Exact steps
- Screenshots placeholders
- Diagrams
- Checklists
- Warnings
- Best practices
- Backup key instructions

Before You Begin: Your Setup Checklist

Before you connect *anything*, complete this simple checklist.

🔍 Pre-Setup Checklist

You will need:

✓ Your **primary YubiKey**

✓ Your **backup YubiKey**

✓ A computer with USB-A or USB-C

✓ Your smartphone (if you use NFC)

✓ Your passwords (or your password manager unlocked)

✓ Access to your email

✓ 10–20 minutes of uninterrupted focus

💡 TIP

Do NOT skip your backup key. Every time you register your primary key on an account, register your backup key at the *same time.*

If you wait, you *will* forget — and your future self will be furious.

The Universal Setup Flow (Works for Almost Every Website)

All secure websites follow nearly the same process.

Use this diagram to visualize what's happening:

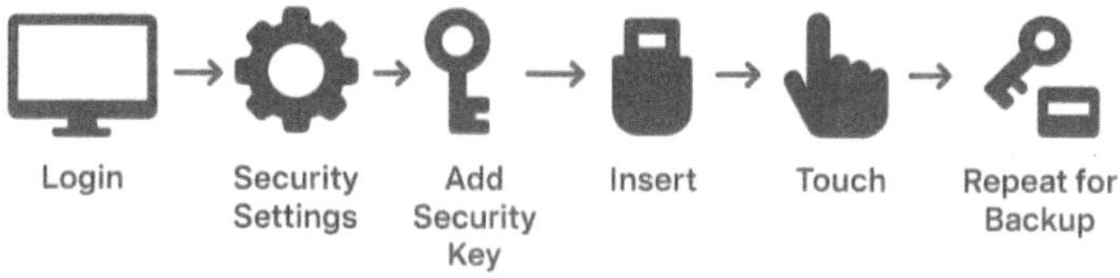

The Setup Steps (Universal Process)

1. **Log in** to your account (bank, email, brokerage, etc.)
2. Navigate to **Security Settings** or **Two-Factor Authentication (2FA)**
3. Select **Add Security Key**
4. Insert your **YubiKey**
5. **Touch the gold circle** when prompted
6. Name your key (example: *"Larry Primary"*)
7. Repeat the process with your **backup key**

That's the whole process in 7 steps.

Setting Up Your Google or Gmail Account

Your email is the beating heart of your digital life.If someone owns your email, they can reset passwords, access your bank, access your investment accounts... everything.

Google is the FIRST account you secure.

Step-by-Step: Adding Your YubiKey to Google

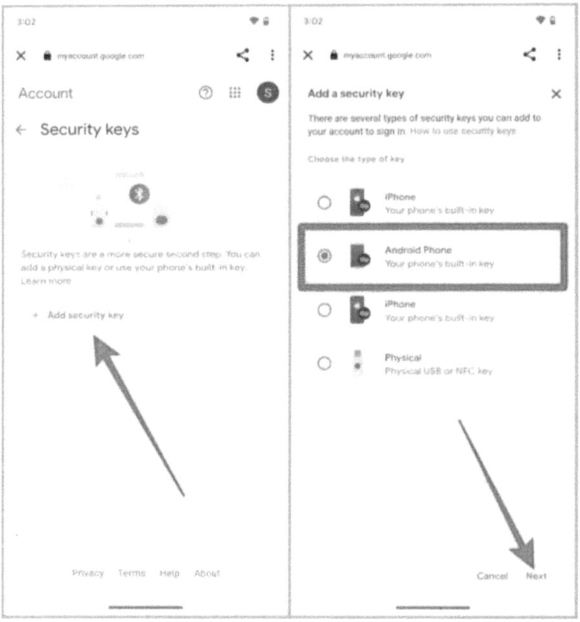

Go to: https://myaccount.google.com/security

Under *"Signing in to Google"* select **2-Step Verification**

- Sign in if prompted
- Scroll to **"Add Security Key"**
- Click **Add security key**
- Insert your **primary YubiKey**
- Touch the gold circle
- Name it:
- *"Name Primary YubiKey"*
- Click **Done**
- Now click **Add Security Keyagain**
- Insert your **backup key**
- Touch it
- Name it:
- *"ChooseName Backup YubiKey"*

⚠ **WARNING: Do NOT delete other 2FA methods yet.**

If something goes wrong and you removed your backup methods, you could lock yourself out.

We will clean them up later in Chapter 8.

Setting Up Your Microsoft Account (Outlook, OneDrive, Windows)

Some banks and brokerages are tied to your Microsoft account for password resets — meaning this one is **critical** too.

- Visit: https://account.microsoft.com/security
- Open **Advanced security options**
- Scroll to **Add a new way to sign in or verify**
- Select **Security Key**
- Choose **USB** (or NFC if phone)
- Insert YubiKey → Touch sensor
- Name it
- Add your **backup key** the same way

Setting Up Your Password Manager (Bitwarden/1Password/LastPass)

If your password manager gets compromised, everything gets compromised.

You *must* lock it down.

Bitwarden Setup

- Log into your vault at: https://vault.bitwarden.com
- Go to **Settings**
- Select **Two-step Login**
- Choose **Security Key (WebAuthn)**
- Click **Manage**
- Insert your **primary YubiKey** and touch
- Name it
- Repeat for backup key

Checklist: Bitwarden Secured

✓ Master password strong

✓ Primary YubiKey registered

✓ Backup YubiKey registered

✓ Recovery code saved offline

✓ Email secured with YubiKey

If all five are ✓, you're armored.

Setting Up Your Bank Accounts (Chase, Bank of America, Wells Fargo)

The #1 goal: protect the money.

Bank support for security keys is improving fast.

Below are the current methods (as of 2025).

Chase

Chase now supports FIDO/WebAuthn for login authentication.

- Log in → Profile & Settings
- Go to **Security & Privacy**
- Select **Two-factor authentication**
- Choose **Security Key**
- Insert your primary key
- Name it
- Add backup key

Bank of America

Bank of America supports security keys for some account types and login paths.

- Log into Online Banking
- Visit **Profile & Settings**

- Find **Advanced Sign-In Security**
- Select **Security Key**
- Add → Insert YubiKey → Touch
- Add backup key

Wells Fargo

As of 2025, Wells Fargo supports FIDO keys for higher-security profiles and brokerage-linked accounts.

- Log in → **Security Center**
- Choose **Two-Step Verification**
- Add **Security Key**
- Insert key
- Add backup

⚠ IMPORTANT BANK WARNING

Many banks will still ask for SMS codes the FIRST time you log in from a new device — even with YubiKey enabled. Don't panic.It doesn't mean the key isn't working.It's simply an additional fraud-screening process.

YubiKey's role is to prevent unauthorized access, not eliminate device-verification procedures.

Setting Up Your Investment Accounts (Vanguard, Fidelity, Schwab)

This is where the big money usually sits — and these platforms are rapidly adopting hardware keys.

Fidelity

Fidelity now supports hardware keys for login verification.

- Log in
- Go to **Security Center**
- Select **Security Key**
- Insert key
- Touch
- Add backup key

Vanguard

Vanguard supports security keys via its **Secure Login** feature.

- Log in
- Navigate to **Security**
- Add **Security Key**

- Insert primary key
- Add backup

Charles Schwab

Schwab supports security keys for their highest-security tier.

- Log in
- Go to **Security Settings**
- Select **Two-factor authentication**
- Add **Security Key**
- Add backup key

Setting Up Your Apple ID (iPhone, iPad, Mac)

Apple has the best implementation in the industry.If you use an iPhone, you *must* set this up.

Steps to Add YubiKey to Apple ID

1. On your iPhone go to:**Settings → Your Name → Password & Security**
2. Tap **Add Security Keys**

3. Insert or tap NFC key
4. Touch the sensor
5. Add 2–6 total keys (Apple requires **minimum 2**)
6. Save
7. Remove old 2FA methods if desired

⚠ **APPLE WARNING**

If you use a MacBook with **Touch ID**, some login flows behave differently.This is normal.

Setting Up Social Media (Facebook, Instagram, Twitter, etc.)

These aren't as critical as your finances — but they *are* critical for identity theft prevention.

All major platforms now support YubiKey-based login.

Chapter Summary: You're Now Armored Up

Check off what you've secured:

✓ **Google / Gmail**

✓ **Microsoft**

✓ **Password Manager**

✔ **Bank Accounts**

✔ **Brokerage / Investment Accounts**

✔ **Apple ID**

✔ **Social Media**

If you've done all of the above…your digital life is now locked behind hardware cryptography.

You've achieved what 99.9% of people never do.

Chapter 5 — Everyday Life With Your YubiKey

How to actually live with it, use it, travel with it, store it, and never lose access to anything.

This chapter is about **real-world usage** — the part most guides forget.You now have your keys set up. Great.

Now what?

Most people never get this far. And even fewer know how to *use* a YubiKey day-to-day without frustration.

This chapter gives you:

- Real-life scenarios
- Daily routines
- How to use your key on every device
- How to avoid lockouts
- Travel & emergency preparedness
- Backup key best practices
- The psychology of feeling secure

Let's begin.

What Happens When You Log In Now

When you visit a secured account, here's the new flow:

- Enter your username/password
- The site prompts you:**"Insert your security key"**
- Plug in your YubiKey
- Touch the gold sensor
- You're in

Total time: **2–4 seconds.**

And here's the important part:

Your password alone cannot unlock anything anymore.The YubiKey is now the deciding factor.

This is what stops hackers cold.

🔍 Diagram: What Logging In Looks Like Now

Figure 5.1 – What Logging In Looks Like Now

Computer → Insert YubiKey → Cryptographic challenge → Verified → Account unlocked]

💡 TIP: You Only Need Your Key When Logging In, Not While Browsing

The YubiKey is **not** constantly communicating.It's only used during authentication.

Once you're logged in, you can:

- unplug it
- put it away
- continue working normally

Admin-grade security, zero annoyance.

How to Use Your YubiKey on Every Device

On a Desktop or Laptop (USB-A or USB-C)

- When the prompt appears
- Insert your key
- Touch it
- Remove when done

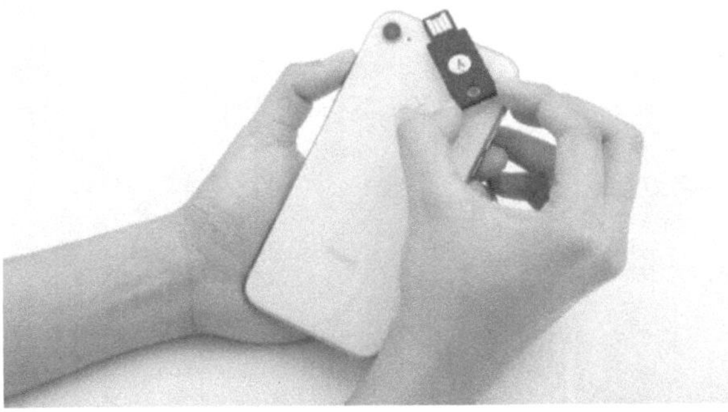

On an iPhone (NFC)

- When prompted, tap the YubiKey to the top/back of the phone
- Wait for the vibration
- You'll be logged in instantly

On an Android Phone (NFC)

- Tap the key against the center-back
- A pop-up appears: "Use security key"
- Touch the gold circle
- You're in

On an iPad or Mac

Depending on the model:

- USB-C → insert key
- Lightning → use a 5Ci or NFC
- MacBook → use USB-C or NFC relay on iPhone if prompted

Apple hides nothing — their prompts walk you through it.

The Only 3 Times You Ever Really Need Your Key

This removes 99% of user anxiety.

You ONLY need your YubiKey when:

1. Logging in from a NEW device

First time only.

After that, you remain trusted longer.

2. Logging in from a NEW browser

Example: Chrome vs Firefox — the browser is treated like a different device.

3. Logging in after clearing cookies

Security keys rely partly on stored trust tokens.

That's it.98% of your daily digital life requires **zero interactions** with the key.

Where to Keep Your Primary Key (Daily Life)

Most people choose one of these:

✓ **On your keychain**

Pros: always with youCons: slightly more wear and tear

✓ **In your wallet**

Pros: always accessibleCons: wallets get sat on; NFC models may trigger occasionally

✓ **In a small pouch or bag you always carry**

Pros: protected, easy to accessCons: don't switch bags often

✓ **At your desk**

Pros: easy for those who work from homeCons: not ideal for travel or unexpected logins

The best choice?

Wherever your house keys live.You rarely lose your house keys.

That habit transfers beautifully.

Where to Keep Your Backup Key

Your backup key MUST be stored safely.

Here are the approved options:

Option A — Home Safe

Best for most people.

Fireproof? Even better.

Option B — Safety Deposit Box

Best for high-net-worth individuals.

Option C — With a Trusted Family Member

For people who want redundancy across physical locations.

Option D — Stored Securely in a Locked File Cabinet

Good enough for many households, especially if bolted down.

🚫 **NEVER store your backup key:**

- In a car glovebox
- In a purse you frequently switch
- In a junk drawer
- In a backpack that isn't always with you

Next to your primary key (defeats the purpose)

What If You Lose Your Primary Key?

Nothing bad happens — **IF you registered your backup.**

Here's what you do:

1. Go get your backup key
2. Log into your accounts using the backup
3. Remove the lost key from each account's security settings
4. Order a new replacement
5. Add the new one as your new backup

Total time: **20–30 minutes.**

⚠ If you lose your only key AND didn't add a backup?

Recovery is painful.

Some services require:

- Passport
- Phone call verification
- Mailing forms
- Waiting days or weeks

This is why this book emphasizes:

Two keys or nothing.

Traveling With Your YubiKey

Your YubiKey is safe to take anywhere — including:

- Airports
- Cruise ships
- Hotels
- International travel
- Out-of-state work trips

It is:

- Waterproof
- Crushproof
- Wash-proof
- TSA-proof

Travel Rule of Thumb

Bring your primary key with you. Leave your backup at home.

If both travel with you and your luggage is stolen, you're exposed.

✈ Travel Packing Checklist

✓ Primary YubiKey on keychain

✓ Backup YubiKey stored safely at home

✓ Password manager logged in before boarding (optional)

✓ Local SIM card or Wi-Fi access for account recovery

The Psychology of Security (What You'll Notice)

People who start using YubiKeys typically report:

1. Less anxiety when logging in

You stop worrying about phishing or password guesses.

2. More confidence using financial accounts

You feel armored — because you are.

3. A sense of control

Instead of "I hope I don't get hacked,"your mindset becomes:**"They'll never get in. Period."**

4. Peace when traveling

Your accounts cannot be breached through your phone, airport Wi-Fi, or hotel networks.

5. Better digital hygiene

People who use YubiKeys naturally:

- reuse fewer passwords
- inspect fewer suspicious emails
- click fewer questionable links
- Security becomes a lifestyle, not a chore.

Everyday YubiKey FAQ

Q: Do I leave the key plugged in all the time?

No. Insert only when prompted.

Q: Can malware steal the YubiKey's secrets?

No.The private keys never leave the hardware — ever.

Q: What if my computer dies?

Your accounts are tied to the YubiKey, not the device.Use any other computer.

Q: What if a thief steals my YubiKey?

Without your password, it's useless.And you can revoke it instantly.

Q: Does it need charging?

No.It contains *no battery* and uses no external power.

Q: How long does a YubiKey last?

5–10 years easily.They are hardened devices.

Chapter Summary: Your New Normal

✓ You now know exactly when you need your key

✓ You know where to store your backup

✓ You know what to do if you lose a key

✓ **You know how to travel with it**

✓ **You understand the psychology and the benefits**

✓ **You are operating at a security level most people will** never **achieve**

The hard part (setup) is behind you.Now you're living with unbreakable digital armor.

Chapter 6 — Backup Keys, Emergency Planning, and Account Recovery

This chapter eliminates the single biggest fear people have about using hardware security keys:"What happens if something goes wrong?"

By the end of this chapter, you will have:

- A complete backup plan
- A recovery plan
- A family/emergency access plan
- A system to avoid lockouts
- A template you can print and store securely
- The exact steps to recover any account

This is the chapter that turns YubiKey security from *strong* into **bulletproof**.

The Golden Rule of YubiKeys

You must remember this:

One YubiKey = RiskTwo YubiKeys = SafetyThree YubiKeys = Indestructible System

Most people will only need **two**, but high-security users (business owners, investors, crypto holders, or people with large retirement accounts) may use three.

Here's the breakdown:

- **Primary Key = Your Daily Driver**
- This is the one you use every day.
- **Backup Key = Stored Safely**
- This key is your lifeline if you lose the primary key.
- **Emergency Key (Optional)**

  This is stored geographically separate:

- A bank safe
- A trust attorney
- A fireproof box in another home
- With a highly trusted family member

This protects you against:

- Fire
- Flood
- Natural disasters
- Tornadoes
- Theft

- Cross-country travel incidents

Setting Up a Bulletproof Backup Key System

You now know that every account must have **both keys registered**.

Here's the system to guarantee you never lose access.

Step 1 — Label Both Keys Clearly

Use a label maker or masking tape + Sharpie.

Examples:

- *Primary – John*
- *Backup - John Safe*
- *Emergency - Safety Deposit Box*

If keys look identical (they usually do), labeling is mandatory.

Step 2 — Create a Secure Storage Plan

Here are the three approved types of secure storage:

1. Home Safe (Most Common)

Fireproof, waterproof, bolted down → ideal.

Store your backup here.

2. Safety Deposit Box

For high-asset households.

Perfect for an emergency key.

3. Distributed Family Trust Plan

Give only the EMERGENCY key to a trusted person.

Never give them the passwords — just the physical key.

Step 3 — Document Your Key Storage (Securely)

Create a simple one-page reference sheet:

📄 **YubiKey Recovery Sheet (Template)**

(Do NOT store this digitally unless encrypted.)

Primary key location: ____________________

Backup key location: _____________________

Emergency key location (optional): _______

Password manager used: __________________

Recovery email: _________________________

Apple ID recovery contacts: _______________

Microsoft recovery email/phone: ___________

Print this, store it in your safe or lockbox.

Step 4 — Teach One Trusted Person the Recovery Process

You do not need to give them passwords.

You only need to:

Explain what a YubiKey is

Show them which key is the emergency key

Tell them where the instructions will be stored

That's it.

This protects you if you become:

Hospitalized

Injured

Incapacitated

Traveling abroad with no access

High-level finance people do this ALL the time.

The Only 3 Ways a YubiKey Emergency Happens

People worry about dozens of hypothetical scenarios.

In reality, there are **only three situations** that matter.

Let's break them down and give you a recovery plan for each.

Scenario 1 — You Lose Your Primary Key

This is the MOST COMMON scenario.

Solution:

1. Retrieve your **backup key**
2. Log into your accounts
3. Remove the lost key
4. Order a replacement
5. Register replacement as your new backup

Scenario 2 — You Lose BOTH Primary and Backup Keys

This is unlikely, but still solvable.

Solution:

Depending on the service, recovery requires:

- Driver's license / passport photo
- Phone verification
- Email verification
- Mailing a form
- Answering stored security questions (if still enabled)

Banks will always recover your identity.Tech companies will almost always recover your identity.

The process takes longer but always works.

Scenario 3 — You Forgot to Register Your Backup Key

This is the scenario we want to avoid.

Solution:

- Contact each service
- Verify identity
- Regain access
- Add TWO keys immediately

Bank & Brokerage Recovery Procedures

Below are the standard recovery processes for major financial institutions.

Chase Recovery

Chase will ask for:

- Full name
- Date of birth
- Last 4 of SSN
- ID verification
- Mailing address confirmation
- Possibly an emailed or mailed recovery code

Never fear: Banks deal with lost authentication devices every day.

Fidelity, Vanguard, and Schwab Recovery

These institutions may require:

Phone verification

Valid ID

Mailing a recovery form

In some cases: notarized signatures

Investment accounts are high stakes, so these extra steps protect YOU.

Tech Account Recovery

Google Recovery

Google recovery is excellent:

- Use backup codes
- Use recovery email
- Use recovery phone
- Identity verification if needed

Apple Recovery

Apple uses:

- Recovery keys
- Trusted phone numbers
- Trusted devices

- Recovery contacts

If all fail, they still offer a slower identity verification path.

Microsoft Recovery

Microsoft may require:

- Recovery email
- Recovery phone
- 30-day waiting period if everything else is missing

This is why you want your backup key registered.

Crypto & High-Security Users (Advanced)

If you hold:

- Crypto
- Gold-backed digital assets
- Private equity digital access
- High-value online accounts

You MUST do the following:

✓ **Create a 3-key system**

Primary, Backup, Emergency

✓ **Store emergency key offsite**

Preferably in a different state.

✓ **Document seed phrases separately**

Your YubiKey protects access to accounts. Your **seed phrase** protects access to the blockchain.

These should NEVER be stored together.

✓ **Use metal plates for seed storage**

Paper burns.Metal doesn't.

Creating a Family "Digital Will"

This is NOT legal advice, but here's a standard approach used by cybersecurity professionals.

A Digital Will Contains:

- Location of backup and emergency YubiKeys
- Password manager master password recovery instructions
- Trusted person contact information
- Asset list (banks, brokerage, crypto wallets)
- Step-by-step instructions for the executor
- This ensures that:
- Your spouse
- Your children
- Your executor
- ...can access critical accounts when needed.

Without this, assets can remain locked for YEARS.

Emergency Checklist (Print This)

If anything goes wrong, do this:

1. Stay calm

Your accounts are still safe.

2. Retrieve your backup or emergency key

3. Log into your password manager

This gives you access to EVERYTHING else.

4. Update each service

Remove lost keys → Add new ones

5. Document the incident

Where, when, what happened(Helps with insurance or bank claims if needed)

6. Rebuild your backup plan immediately

Never operate with only one key.

Chapter Summary

After this chapter, you now have:

✓ **A complete backup + recovery system**

✔ **A secure storage plan**

✔ **A family emergency plan**

✔ **A digital will structure**

✔ **A step-by-step guide for every disaster scenario**

✔ **Peace of mind that you will NEVER be locked out**

This is the chapter that transforms beginners into **professionals**.

You now have the same redundancy and security structure as:

- Corporate executives
- Financial advisors
- IT security officers
- High-net-worth individuals
- Crypto custodians

You are ahead of 99.99% of the world.

Chapter 7 — Protecting Your Entire Family With YubiKeys

You've secured yourself. Now it's time to secure the people you love.

This chapter is about building a **family-wide protection system** that prevents:

- Identity theft
- Bank account fraud
- Social media takeovers
- Email compromises
- School account breaches
- SIM swaps
- Unauthorized online purchases

A family security plan is one of the greatest gifts you can give to your spouse, your children, and your legacy.

Let's build it.

Why Families Need YubiKeys More Than Individuals

When one family member gets hacked, it often spreads:

Your spouse's email may be the recovery email for your accounts

Your child's school account may be connected to your family Apple ID

Your home finances may depend on multiple shared logins

Social media accounts of family members become impersonation targets

Phones get stolen, lost, or broken

Kids install apps without understanding the risks

Security is not an individual sport.

Your family is only as secure as its weakest account.

The Family Security Pyramid

Here's the structure for a fully protected digital household:

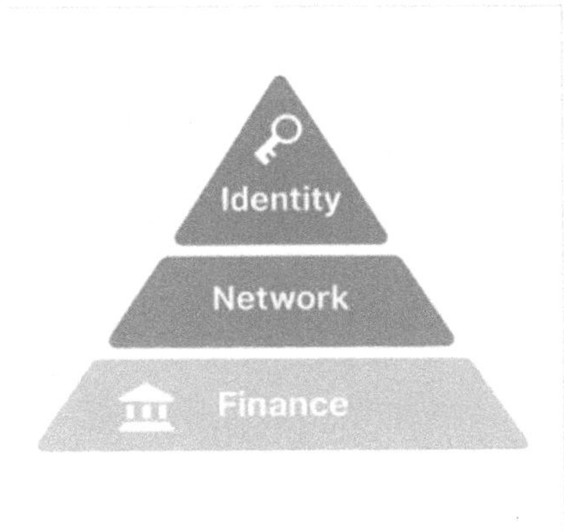

Top Layer — Parents / Heads of Household

- Financial accounts

- Password managers
- Apple IDs / Google accounts
- Email / social media
- Tax accounts
- Insurance accounts

Middle Layer — Teenagers

- Email
- Phone security
- Social media
- School accounts
- Gaming accounts
- App Store purchases

Bottom Layer — Children

- Locked-down devices
- Child Apple IDs
- Restricted app access
- No password reuse
- Parent-administered YubiKey accounts (optional)

The Family YubiKey Package (What to Buy)

To secure a whole household, here's the recommended purchase plan:

For a Two-Adult Household

Each Adult Needs:

1 Primary Key

1 Backup Key

So: **4 total keys**

Optional:

1 Emergency Key stored in a safe(Brings total to 5 keys)

For Households With Teens

Give each teen:

1 Primary Key (on keychain or in desk drawer)

1 Parent-held Backup Key

So: +2 keys per teen.

For Young Children (Under 12)

They do **not** need their own keys.Instead:

- Lock their devices
- Use parental controls
- Secure parent accounts
- Use password manager for shared family logins

The Family Setup Flow (Step-by-Step)

Here's the complete system.

Step 1 — Secure Parent Accounts First

Parents are the backbone.Secure all:

- Bank accounts
- Brokerage accounts
- Tax accounts
- Email accounts
- Password managers
- Apple IDs
- Microsoft accounts
- Google accounts

- Insurance accounts
- Credit card logins

When parents are protected, the entire family becomes more resistant to fraud.

Step 2 — Secure Teen Accounts

Teenagers are at higher risk of:

- SIM-swapping
- Social media hacks
- Malware from games
- Lost phones
- Phishing attacks
- Fake giveaways (crypto/NFT scams, gaming skins, etc.)

Give each teen:

- A **primary YubiKey**
- A parent-held **backup key**

Then secure:

Critical Teen Accounts

- Email
- iCloud / Apple ID
- Google account
- Instagram
- Snapchat
- TikTok
- Gaming platforms (PlayStation, Xbox, Steam)
- School accounts (Google Classroom, Canvas, etc.)

Step 3 — Protect Shared Family Logins

Examples:

- Netflix
- Amazon
- Disney+
- YouTube TV
- Smart home devices
- Wi-Fi router login
- Security cameras
- Most of these support:

- Strong passwords
- 2FA
- Password manager autofill
- Parents maintain the master keys.

Special Cases: Securing Elderly Parents

This is extremely important.

Elderly individuals are prime targets of:

- Phone scams
- Tech support scams
- Banking fraud
- Facebook impersonations
- Medicare / SSA phishing

Here's the solution:

For each elderly parent:

- 1 Primary YubiKey
- 1 Caregiver-Held Backup Key

Then lock down:

- Email
- Bank accounts
- Medicare.gov
- Social Security
- Pharmacy portals
- MyChart / medical portals
- Password manager

Pro Tip:

Add yourself as a **trusted recovery contact** for:

- Apple
- Google
- Microsoft
- Banking apps

This prevents catastrophic loss of access.

Family Emergency Planning

Create a "Family Digital Emergency Kit" inside a fireproof safe.

This contains:

- Backup YubiKeys
- Emergency passwords

- Recovery codes
- A printed Family Recovery Sheet
- Executor access instructions
- Trusted contact list
- A sealed envelope with the password manager master password (optional)

What the Family Recovery Sheet Looks Like

Family Digital Security Sheet

Parent 1 primary key location: __________

Parent 1 backup key location: __________

Parent 2 primary key location: __________

Parent 2 backup key location: __________

Teen key locations: ______________________

Emergency key location: __________________

Safe combination / access instructions: ___

Trusted contact names: _________________

Store this in:

A home safe

A lawyer's office

A safety deposit box

Never store digitally unless encrypted.

Teaching Kids and Teens About Security

You do NOT need to teach them cryptography. You teach them *habits*.

The 10-Minute Teen Security Lesson

Teach them:

- Never share passwords
- Never click unknown links
- Use a password manager
- If the YubiKey prompt appears—use the key
- Report suspicious messages immediately
- Treat your phone like your wallet
- Never install unknown apps
- Don't join random Wi-Fi networks
- Don't share verification codes
- Lock your phone with a strong passcode

Kids learn fast. Security becomes normal.

The Family Security Checklist (Print This)

Parents Secured

✓ Email

✓ Banks

✓ Investments

✓ Apple IDs / Google

✓ Password manager

✓ Insurance portals

✓ Tax accounts

Teens Secured

✓ Email

✓ Social media

✓ School accounts

✓ Gaming accounts

✓ iCloud/Google accounts

Household Secured

✓ Wi-Fi router

✓ Smart home devices

✓ Shared logins

✓ Streaming services

✓ Emergency planning

Backup System

✓ Backup YubiKeys for all adults

✓ Parent-held teen backups

✓ Emergency key

✓ Printed recovery instructions

This is how families become unhackable.

Chapter Summary

You now have:

✓ **A full family YubiKey deployment plan**

✓ **Backup keys for every adult and teen**

✓ **Emergency keys stored securely**

✓ **A family digital emergency kit**

✓ **Elderly parent protection**

✓ **Teen and child account protection**

✓ **Household-wide security best practices**

You haven't just protected yourself.

You've protected:

- Your spouse
- Your children
- Your parents
- Your digital legacy

This is what modern digital leadership looks like.

Chapter 8 — Cleaning Up Old Security Methods (Eliminating Weak Links)

Now that your YubiKeys are fully set up and your family is protected, it's time to eliminate the old, weak security methods that hackers depend on.

This chapter is **ESSENTIAL.**

Right now, your accounts are likely still allowing:

- SMS text codes
- Old phone numbers
- Unused authenticator apps
- Forgotten backup codes
- Old recovery emails
- Secondary devices you don't even use
- Weak security questions
- Untrustworthy browsers

These are **loopholes** that can be exploited — even if you have YubiKeys enabled.

We are about to close them forever.

Why Cleanup Matters (This Is Where People Slip Up)

Hackers LOVE old backup methods.

They don't need your YubiKey if they can:

SIM swap your phone

Access your old email account

Trigger a password reset to a backup phone

Use old recovery codes you forgot about

Log in from a trusted-but-forgotten device

Think of this cleanup as draining all the swamp water where threats hide.

You are not fully protected until ALL weak recovery methods are purged.

The Cleanup Checklist (Print This)

These are the old methods you must inspect and disable, where possible:

❌ **SMS codes**

❌ **Phone call verification**

❌ **Old phone numbers**

❌ **Old email addresses**

❌ **Authenticator apps you no longer use**

❌ **Security questions (mother's maiden name, etc.)**

❌ **Old browsers listed as "trusted"**

❌ **Old laptops/phones still registered**

❌ **Backup codes stored on your devices**

✓ **Replace every one of these with:**

YubiKeys + Password Manager + Trusted Emails ONLY.

Cleaning Up Google / Gmail (Step-by-Step)

Go to: https://myaccount.google.com/security

Step 1 — Remove old 2FA methods

Under *"2-Step Verification"*:

- Remove **Authenticator Apps**

- Remove **Backup Codes** (generate new if needed)
- Remove **SMS**
- Remove **Voice call**
- Remove **Unused security keys**

Step 2 — Remove old devices

Under *"Your devices"*:

- Remove every device you don't recognize
- Remove old laptops
- Remove old phones
- Remove browsers you no longer use

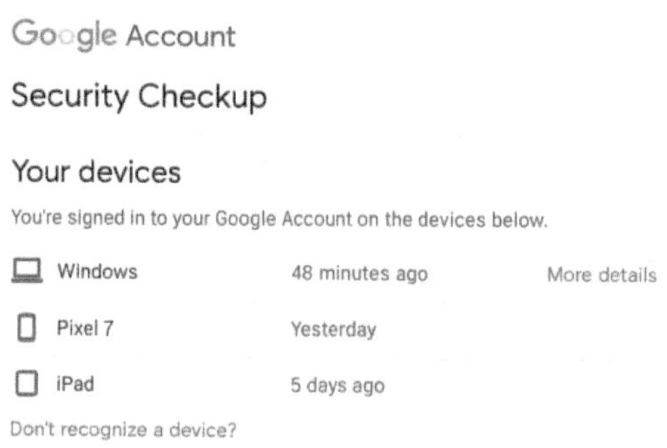

Step 3 — Clean recovery emails and phones

Under *"Ways we can verify it's you"*:

- Delete old email addresses
- Delete unused phone numbers

Keep **only ONE phone** and **ONE recovery email**

Step 4 — Secure backup codes (optional)

If you choose to keep backup codes:

- Print them
- Store in a safe
- Never store them digitally
- Never store them in your email

Cleaning Up Apple ID

Go to: **Settings → Your Name → Password & Security**

Step 1 — Remove old devices

Scroll to *Devices*:Tap → Remove all devices you no longer use.

Step 2 — Remove old phone numbers

Under **Trusted Phone Numbers**:Delete every number except your current one.

Step 3 — Disable old 2FA methods

Once security keys are enabled:

- Remove authenticator apps
- Remove backup phone numbers

Apple does not use SMS codes as backups once security keys are enabled — this is good.

Cleaning Up Microsoft Accounts

Go to: https://account.microsoft.com/security

Remove:

- Authenticator app (if not needed)
- SMS codes
- Voice calls
- Backup emails
- Unknown devices

- Old trusted devices
- Microsoft is notorious for piling up old authentication methods — clear them all.

Cleaning Up Password Managers

This is easy but critical.

1Password / Bitwarden / LastPass cleanup

Remove:

- Old devices
- Old fingerprint registrations
- Old TOTP apps
- SMS fallback
- Backup email accounts you no longer use

Your **password manager** is the master key — keep only the minimum safe methods.

Cleaning Up Banks & Brokerages

Banks hide old security methods deeper in their settings.

Here's where to find them:

Chase

Go to:

Profile & Settings → Security & Privacy → Additional Security

Remove:

- Old phone numbers
- Old devices
- Outdated 2FA methods
- Once YubiKey/WebAuthn is enabled, eliminate SMS.

Bank of America

Go to:

Security Center → Manage SafePass / Extra Security

Turn OFF:

- SMS codes
- Email codes
- Mobile app verification (if redundant)

Fidelity / Schwab / Vanguard

Under Security settings:

- Disable SMS
- Remove old devices
- Remove old trusted browsers
- Regenerate backup codes (store offline)
- Investment accounts are high-target — treat these with extra care.

Cleaning Up Social Media (Identity Theft Prevention)

Identity theft usually begins with:

- Email
- Facebook
- Instagram
- Twitter
- TikTok

Lock these down.

Remove:

- SMS codes
- Authenticator apps
- Past devices
- Past browsers
- Unknown logins
- Third-party app access

Most social hacks occur through **old sessions** left active for years.

Disable everything that isn't your current phone/computer.

Cleaning Up Your Phone (Critical)

Phones often contain:

- Old apps with permissions
- Malware from unknown apps
- Trusted Wi-Fi networks
- Saved passwords
- Auto-fill vulnerabilities

Do this:

iPhone Cleanup Checklist

✓ Remove old devices

✓ Reset Network Settings (optional)

✓ Disable "Allow Apps to Request to Track"

✓ Review app permissions

✓ Remove old Apple IDs

✓ Remove unused apps

✓ Turn off autofill for passwords if using password manager

Android Cleanup Checklist

✓ Remove old Google accounts

✓ Disable unknown app installations

✓ Review permissions (camera, mic, location)

✓ Remove apps not used in 90+ days

✓ Disable manufacturer cloud services you don't use

The Final Sweep: Your Browser

The browser is the #1 attack target for phishing.

Do this:

Browser Cleanup Checklist

In Chrome / Edge / Brave:

❌ Delete ALL saved passwords

❌ Turn OFF autofill

❌ Remove old profiles

❌ Clear "Trusted Devices"

❌ Remove rogue extensions

❌ Delete unknown cookies / sessions

✓ Enable password manager extension instead

Extensions to Remove Immediately:

- Coupon extensions
- Download managers
- Unknown VPNs
- Anything labeled "assistant"
- Anything that injects ads

- Crypto wallet extensions you don't use

What NOT to Remove

Do **not** remove the following unless you're absolutely sure:

✓ **Your password manager's 2FA**

✓ **YubiKey registrations**

✓ **Trusted devices you CURRENTLY use**

✓ **Recovery email**

✓ **Recovery phone number**

If in doubt, keep it.

Chapter Summary

You have now ✓ Eliminated SMS vulnerabilities

✓ **Removed old devices and browsers**

✓ **Deleted outdated 2FA methods**

✓ **Cleaned up dangerous recovery methods**

✓ **Secured phones and browsers**

✓ **Locked down bank and investment accounts**

✔ **Purged old authenticator apps**

✔ **Secured your identity across all services**

This is the point where your security posture becomes **airtight**.

Hackers rely on your old, forgotten methods — but you just erased their footholds.

Chapter 9 — The YubiKey Troubleshooting & Survival Guide

This chapter is your insurance policy. If anything ever goes wrong—anything at all—this is the guide that gets you back in control within minutes.

We're going to cover:

- Common YubiKey issues
- Browser issues
- Phone issues
- Website issues
- Backup key failures
- Lost key scenarios
- "Device not recognized" errors
- Travel issues
- Operating system problems
- USB port and NFC troubleshooting
- A visual decision tree for quick diagnosis
- A full emergency flowchart
- No stress.No panic.Just solutions.

The Golden Rule of Troubleshooting

Before anything else:

99% of YubiKey problems are *not* YubiKey problems.They're browser or device issues.

The YubiKey almost never fails.

It's the device, website, or browser that needs attention.

Quick Troubleshooting Flowchart

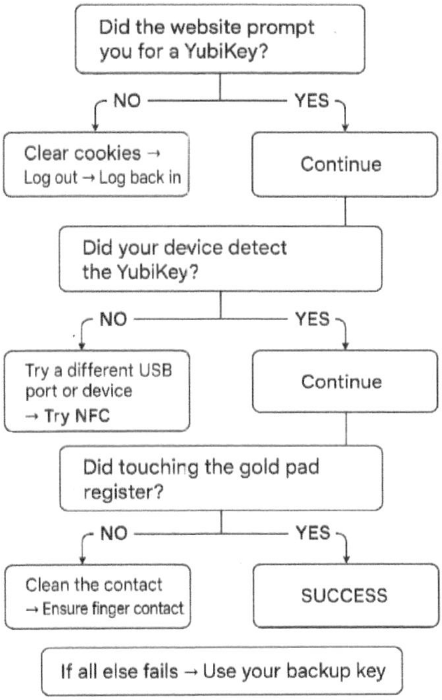

When Your Computer Doesn't Recognize the YubiKey

This is common on:

- Older USB ports
- Dirty or damaged USB ports
- Laptops running outdated OS versions
- Browsers missing WebAuthn support

Fixes:

1. Try a different USB port

Side ports often work better than back ports.USB-C is more reliable than USB-A.

2. Restart your browser

Chrome, Firefox, Safari, and Edge sometimes need a fresh handshake.

3. Restart your computer

This resets USB power states.

4. Test your key at:

https://demo.yubico.com/webauthn

If it works there → your key is fine.

5. Clean the USB contacts

Use a microfiber cloth or alcohol wipe.

When NFC Isn’t Working on Your Phone

NFC issues come from:

- Phone cases
- Adhesive wallets
- Magnets
- Wrong tap location
- Disabled NFC settings

Fixes:

1. Remove the phone case

Thick cases block NFC entirely.

2. Tap in the right location

iPhone:**Top rear near the camera**

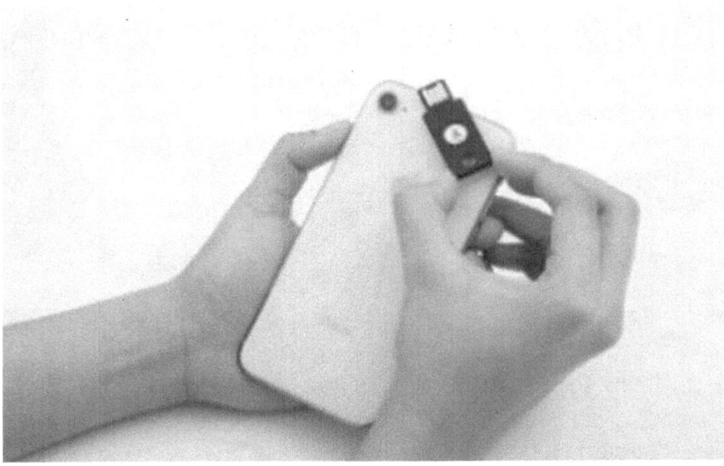

Android:**Varies—usually center back**

3. Enable NFC

iPhone: always onAndroid:**Settings → Connected Devices → NFC toggle**

4. Try a different angle

A flat tap is best.

When the Website Rejects the Key

This happens when:

- You added the wrong key

- The service uses a specific authentication method
- Your browser is blocking WebAuthn
- You're using an unsupported browser mode

Fixes:

1. Make sure you're using the same key you registered

Check the label: *Primary* vs *Backup*.

2. Disable incognito/private mode

Some sites block WebAuthn in private mode.

3. Switch browsers

- Chrome
- Firefox
- Safari
- Edge

If one fails, another usually works instantly.

4. Disable browser extensions

Especially:

- Ad blockers
- Script blockers
- Privacy extensions
- VPN browser plugins

5. Update your browser

Old browsers = rejected WebAuthn signals.

When the Touch Sensor Isn't Responding

This rarely happens, but when it does:

1. Make sure your finger is touching the gold circle

Bare skin is required. Gloves won't work.

2. Clean the sensor pad

Oil or residue can reduce sensitivity.

3. Insert the key fully

If the key wiggles, the connection may be unstable.

4. Try another USB port or device

This isolates the problem.

If none of these work →Use your **backup key** and replace the primary.

YubiKeys have no moving parts. A dead sensor is extremely rare.

"Unknown Device" or "Unrecognized Browser" Problems

Most common causes:

- VPN or proxy changing your IP
- Using a new device
- Using a new browser
- Clearing cookies recently
- Chrome profile resets

- Private browsing mode

Fixes:

1. Turn off VPN temporarily

Some banks block login attempts from VPNs.

2. Try logging in without private mode

WebAuthn may not work in incognito.

3. Log in using your PRIMARY device

Your phone/laptop will have the best trust history.

4. Let the bank run its verification

Even with a YubiKey, banks often require a one-time SMS or email for new devices.

This is normal and NOT a security downgrade.

When Traveling (International Troubleshooting)

If something fails while traveling:

1. Use your backup login methods stored in your password manager

Your master password + YubiKey = total access.

2. Use your phone's browser instead of hotel Wi-Fi computers

Never use public computers.

3. Use cellular data instead of public Wi-Fi

More secure and more reliable.

4. Time zones may delay SMS fallback codes

(Again, normal. SMS is being phased out anyway.)

5. If USB ports look suspicious

Use **NFC only**.

When You Lose a Key (Fast Response Protocol)

Here's the protocol to follow **immediately**.

🚨 If you lose your PRIMARY key:

1. Retrieve your **backup key**
2. Log into all important accounts
3. Remove the missing key
4. Order a replacement
5. Register the new key as your new backup

Done.

🚨 If you lose BOTH keys:

- Log into your password manager (if possible)
- Begin account-by-account identity recovery
- Contact your bank FIRST
- Contact your email provider SECOND
- Reset your security setup with new keys

This takes longer, but it always works.

🚨 If your key is physically stolen:

Your accounts are still safe because:

- The thief doesn't know your password
- They cannot unlock the key
- The key cannot be cloned

Just:

- Remove the stolen key from all accounts
- Use your backup key to remain secure
- Replace the stolen key within 48 hours

99% of Problems Are Solved With These Quick Fixes

Here's your **Lightning Troubleshooting Checklist**:

✔ **Try another USB port**

✔ **Switch to another browser**

✔ **Restart the browser**

✔ **Restart the device**

✓ Use NFC instead of USB

✓ Disable VPN temporarily

✓ Disable extensions

✓ Test at demo.yubico.com

✓ Try your backup key

If the backup key works → the primary key may need replacement.

If NEITHER key works → browser or device issue, not the key.

When to Contact Yubico Support

Very rarely, you may need to contact support.

Contact Yubico when:

- The gold sensor doesn't respond on ANY device
- USB detection fails everywhere
- The key physically breaks
- You see obvious hardware damage
- The key won't authenticate on demo.yubico.com

Yubico's support is extremely good.

Chapter Summary

You now have:

✓ **A complete troubleshooting flowchart**

✓ **Fixes for all major device and browser issues**

✓ **NFC troubleshooting instructions**

✓ **A protocol for lost keys**

✓ **Travel troubleshooting techniques**

✓ **A lightning-fast problem resolution checklist**

✓ **The confidence that NOTHING can lock you out**

Most people fear hardware keys because they fear "getting stuck."

You now have the knowledge, tools, and backup structures to remain unstoppable.

Between Chapters 6 and 9 combined, you have:

- Redundancy
- Recovery
- Emergency access
- Troubleshooting
- Backup strategy
- Disaster-proof planning

You are now operating at the **highest level of digital security available to consumers**.

Chapter 10 — The Ultimate Financial Security Upgrade (Beyond YubiKey)

You've secured your logins. Now it's time to secure your identity, your credit, your taxes, your healthcare, your home network, and every financial pathway that criminals exploit.

This chapter is about **locking down your entire financial life** so thoroughly that even if someone got your Social Security number, your date of birth, and your address, they still couldn't take a single dollar from you.

We're going to cover:

- Credit freezes
- Bank account lockdowns
- IRS security features
- Social Security / Medicare protection
- Tax return fraud prevention
- Home network defenses
- Financial document security
- Protecting your investments and retirement accounts
- Fraud alerts and monitoring
- How to build a "Fort Knox" financial perimeter

This is the final transformation from "safe" to **unhackable**.

Why Securing Your Identity Matters Even With YubiKeys

YubiKeys protect your ACCOUNTS.

But identity theft targets:

- Your Social Security Number
- Your tax return
- Your credit file
- Your bank-to-bank transfers
- Your student loans
- Your investment accounts
- Your insurance payouts

Once a criminal has your identity, they attempt:

- Opening new credit cards
- Filing fake tax returns
- Taking out loans
- Draining retirement accounts
- Signing up for benefits
- Applying for unemployment under your name

This chapter stops ALL of that.

Freeze Your Credit (The #1 Most Important Step)

A **credit freeze** is the single most powerful financial protection you can enable.

A credit freeze makes it **legally impossible** for anyone to:

- Open a loan
- Open a credit card
- Finance a car
- Open a bank account
- Apply for a mortgage
- ...in your name WITHOUT lifting the freeze.

It does NOT affect:

- Your credit score
- Your existing cards
- Your mortgage
- Your bank accounts

It ONLY protects you.

Freeze your credit at all four bureaus:

1. Equifax (most important)

https://my.equifax.com

2. Experian

https://www.experian.com/freeze

3. TransUnion

https://www.transunion.com/credit-freeze

4. Innovis

https://www.innovis.com/personal/securityFreeze

innovis

Experian™
A world of insight

EQUIFAX

TransUnion

📌 **All Freezes are free.**

What a freeze prevents:

- Criminals opening loans
- Criminals raising your credit line
- Criminals opening cell phone accounts
- Criminals creating utilities in your name
- Criminals applying for government benefits

Credit freeze alone blocks 80% of identity theft attempts.

Add Fraud Alerts (Optional Layer)

A fraud alert tells institutions:

- "Verify this person with extra scrutiny before approving anything."

There are three types:

1. Basic Fraud Alert — 1 year (free)

2. Extended Fraud Alert — 7 years (requires identity theft report)

3. Active Duty Alert — for military

Fraud alerts propagate across all three major credit bureaus.

Lock Down Your IRS Account

Tax refund fraud is one of the most common identity theft crimes.

Protect yourself:

Step 1 — Create an IRS online account

https://www.irs.gov/payments/your-online-account

Step 2 — Enable extra verification

IRS uses "ID.me" with facial recognition, which is incredibly secure.

Step 3 — Get an IRS IP PIN

This is one of the **strongest protections you can enable**.

An IRS IP PIN:

Is a 6-digit identity protection code

REQUIRED to file your tax return

Prevents criminals from filing fake tax returns

Changes every year

Only you and the IRS know it

Without your IP PIN, nobody can file a tax return under your name.

This stops:

- Refund theft
- Fraudulent stimulus claims
- Fraudulent dependent claims
- Fake returns

Lock Down Your Social Security & Medicare Accounts

These are extremely high-value targets for identity thieves.

Secure your Social Security Account

1. Go to https://www.ssa.gov/myaccount
2. Create or log in

3. Enable **extra security**
4. Add a **YubiKey** if supported OR secure with strong 2FA
5. Lock down recovery methods

Secure your Medicare.gov Account

- Go to https://www.medicare.gov
- Create or log in
- Enable strong authentication
- Secure your email (with YubiKey)
- Never use SMS as the primary method

Medical identity theft is REAL — criminals use stolen identities to obtain drugs, treatments, or commit Medicare fraud in your name.

Secure Your Bank Transfers & Wire Settings

Even with YubiKeys, make sure your bank has maximum safeguards enabled.

Turn on these settings (if available):

✔ **Wire transfer limits**

✓ Wire transfer alerts

✓ ACH transfer alerts

✓ Login notifications

✓ New device notifications

✓ High-risk transaction alerts

✓ Require verbal confirmation (for large transfers)

Configure Alerts to Your Advantage

Set your bank to send notifications via:

- Email
- Push notifications
- Banking app alerts

Never rely solely on SMS.

Secure Your Retirement Accounts (401k / IRA)

These accounts contain LIFE-CHANGING amounts of money.

Secure them with:

- YubiKeys
- Strong password manager
- Email secured with YubiKey
- No SMS fallback
- No old devices in the login list
- Transaction verification alerts

Add "Trusted Contacts" if available

- Some plan custodians allow:
- "Trusted Contacts"
- "Account guardians"
- "Incapacity access"
- Use these options.

Freeze ChexSystems (Bank Account Fraud Prevention)

Criminals open fraudulent checking accounts to:

- Launder money
- Commit check fraud
- Create synthetic identities

- Freeze your ChexSystems:
- https://www.chexsystems.com

This blocks anyone from opening bank accounts in your name.

Freeze LexisNexis (The Secret Mega Database)

LexisNexis holds huge amounts of personal data used by:

- Insurance companies
- Loan companies
- Background checks
- Government agencies
- A LexisNexis freeze prevents:
- Fraudulent insurance claims
- Criminals opening accounts
- Criminals impersonating you

Freeze here:

https://consumer.risk.lexisnexis.com

Secure Your Home Network (Your First Firewall)

A YubiKey protects logins.Your home network protects the INVISIBLE layer.

Let's make your home network military-grade:

Step 1 — Change Router Password

Do this immediately if you're using:

- "admin"
- "password"
- "123456"
- Default credentials
- Use your password manager to generate a strong password.

Step 2 — Use WPA3 (or at least WPA2)

Open networks are vulnerable to:

- Packet sniffing
- Credential theft
- Device impersonation

Step 3 — Name Your Wi-Fi Something Neutral

Never use:

- Your last name
- Your address
- Your phone number
- Your router brand

Use something like:**PineTree_5G** or **Skyway_Network**

Step 4 — Separate IoT Devices

Smart TVs, cameras, plugs, lights, vacuums → insecure.

Put them on a **guest network** so they can't reach your:

- Phones
- Laptops
- Banking devices

Step 5 — Enable Router Firewalls

Most routers have these built in:

- SPI firewall
- DoS protection
- Traffic monitoring

Turn them on.

Optional: Use a Hardware Firewall (Firewalla, UniFi, etc.)

A dedicated firewall device gives:

- IP blocking
- Geo-blocking
- Intrusion detection
- Device isolation
- Better network segmentation

This is professional-grade security.

Secure Your Financial Documents

Make sure:

✓ **Tax returns are encrypted**

✓ **Bank statements are stored offline or in password manager**

✓ **Sensitive PDFs are password-protected**

✓ **Backups are stored on encrypted drives**

The Annual Financial Security Audit (Print This)

Once per year, perform this audit:

Financial Accounts

✓ Banks

✓ Brokerage accounts

✓ Retirement accounts

✓ Insurance portals

Identity Protection

✓ Freezes still active

✓ IP PIN renewed

✓ LexisNexis frozen

✓ ChexSystems frozen

Digital Security

✓ YubiKeys tested

✓ Backup keys verified

✓ Browsers updated

✓ Password manager audited

✓ Old devices removed

Home Network

✓ Firewalls on

✓ IoT isolated

✓ Wi-Fi updated

✓ Router firmware updated

Documents

✓ Encrypted

✓ Backed up

✓ Organized

This yearly audit keeps you secure indefinitely.

Chapter Summary

You have now implemented:

✓ **Credit freezes**

✓ **Identity protection**

✓ **IRS IP PIN**

✓ **Social Security security**

✓ **Retirement account hardening**

✓ **ChexSystems & LexisNexis freezes**

✓ **Home network security**

✓ **Document encryption**

✓ **Financial alerts**

✓ **A yearly audit**

With this chapter completed, you now have a **complete financial security perimeter**.

You are operating at a level of security normally reserved for high-net-worth individuals, cybersecurity professionals, and executives.

This is the modern equivalent of Fort Knox.

Chapter 11 — Advanced YubiKey Tips, Tricks & Expert-Level Secrets

You now know everything required to be more secure than 99.99% of people.This chapter takes you into the final 0.01% — the domain of cybersecurity pros, system architects, and high-net-worth digital security setups.

These techniques are optional.You don't *need* them...But if you implement even a handful, you will be running a system that is as close to **unhackable** as modern consumer technology allows.

Let's unlock the expert-level layer.

The "Three-Key Rotation System" (Pro Method)

This is the highest level of YubiKey redundancy used in corporate security.

It works like this:

Key A — Daily Driver (Primary)

Always on your person or keychain.

Key B — Home Backup

Stored in safe/fireproof box.

Key C — Offsite / Geographically Separate Emergency Key

Safety deposit box / trusted family member / office vault.

Why This Works

It protects against:

- House fire
- Burglary
- Travel loss
- Natural disaster
- Total device failure
- Simultaneous primary + backup loss

This is as resilient as security gets.

Bind YubiKeys to Multiple Browsers & Profiles

Most people only register their keys with:

- Chrome
- Safari
- Firefox

But here's an expert move:

Register your YubiKey in ALL browsers you use.

This prevents lockouts when:

- A browser profile becomes corrupted
- A plugin breaks WebAuthn
- A browser update glitches
- You need emergency access on a different app

Example Setup:

- Chrome Profile 1 → registered
- Chrome Profile 2 → registered
- Firefox → registered
- Safari → registered
- Edge → registered

This gives you **5 access paths** instead of one.

The "Device Trust Map" Technique

This is a map of all devices that can be used to authenticate you.

Example:

Primary Device Trust Map

- Your laptop (trusted device)
- Your main phone
- Your tablet

- Your backup laptop (optional)

Pro Tip:

At least **two devices** should be capable of login + 2FA.

If your laptop dies and your phone is lost at the same time (rare, but possible), you can still authenticate using a trusted tablet or backup computer.

Master Your Password Manager + YubiKey Workflow

This is the part that feels like magic.

The Ideal Login Flow:

- Unlock password manager
- Autofill username/password
- Insert YubiKey
- Access granted

Total time: **under 5 seconds.**

Expert Trick:

Use your password manager to store recovery URLs, emergency instructions, and security contacts.

Create a secure folder called:

- **/Security / Emergency Access**

Store:

- Recovery URLs
- IRS IP PIN instructions
- Backup email credentials
- Bank support phone numbers
- List of where keys are registered

This centralizes all security info behind your YubiKey-protected vault.

Offline Security: How to Protect Yourself Without Internet

This is for:

- Traveling
- Natural disasters
- Power outages
- Situations where the internet is compromised

Print the following (store in safe):

- Backup codes
- Password manager emergency kit
- Bank fraud hotline numbers
- Credit bureau freeze/unfreeze hotlines
- IRS IP PIN instructions
- Master YubiKey recovery sheet

This allows you to recover your identity *even if the entire internet is down around you.*

Protecting "Hidden Accounts" Most People Forget About

Here are the accounts hackers target because most people forget them exist:

Forgotten Accounts to Secure:

✓ eBay

Hackers use it to scam buyers under your identity.

✓ PayPal

Often linked to bank accounts.

✓ Venmo / Cash App / PayPal

Financial apps MUST be secured.

✓ Amazon

Biggest financial gateway for most households.

✓ Credit card portals

Chase, AmEx, Discover, Capital One.

✓ Pharmacy portals

Walgreens, CVS, mail-order pharmacies.

✓ Utility portals

Electric, water, gas, city services.

✓ Insurance portals

Life, auto, home, health.

✓ Real estate accounts

✓Mortgage providers, escrow accounts, HOA portals.

Expert Tip:

Create a password manager folder called **"Forgotten Accounts"** and audit it annually.

Using Multiple YubiKeys Across Multiple Accounts Efficiently

Some people ask:

"Should I use a different YubiKey for each account?"

No.

One key can protect hundreds of accounts. And your backup key mirrors all the same registrations.

When to diversify keys:

- If you operate a business
- If you manage other people's accounts
- If you want a separate "financial-only" key
- If you want compartmentalized risk

Example:

Setup Option A (Simple — recommended for most)

Primary key → All accountsBackup key → All accounts

Setup Option B (Compartmentalized)

Key #1 → Personal / FamilyKey #2 → Business / WorkKey #3 → Developer / Admin accounts

This keeps breaches isolated.

Using a YubiKey Without USB Ports (Pro Workarounds)

If you're on:

- A locked-down work computer
- A tablet with no USB ports
- A Chromebook
- A public library computer (never recommended)

Use these tricks:

1. Use NFC authentication

Phones always support YubiKey via NFC.

2. Use your phone as a WebAuthn authenticator

Some services let you authenticate through your phone → which uses your YubiKey.

3. Use USB-C to USB-A adapters

A $6 adapter turns a USB-A YubiKey into USB-C, and vice versa.

4. Use Yubico Authenticator (Advanced OTP Mode)

Certain YubiKeys support OTP slots and TOTP generation.

Expert-Level Backup Key Naming Strategy

Most people name their keys:

Key 1

Key 2

But pros use names that prevent confusion and align with future audits.

Perfect naming scheme:

YK-Primary-2025-John

YK-Backup-HomeSafe-2025

YK-Emergency-DepositBox-2025

This eliminates ambiguity when reviewing security dashboards on:

- Google
- Apple
- Microsoft
- Banks
- Password manager

You'll never question which key is which.

How to Replace Keys Without Breaking Anything

Here is the least stressful replacement procedure.

Step 1 — Register new key as "backup"

Do this for *all* accounts.

Step 2 — Make sure login works everywhere

Step 3 — Remove old primary key

Step 4 — Promote backup key to primary

Step 5 — Add second backup key if needed

This "rolling replacement" ensures zero downtime.

The 5-Minute Quarterly Security Routine (Expert-Level)

Once every 90 days:

✓ **Test both YubiKeys**

Login to any YubiKey-required service.

✓ **Verify that backup key still works**

Use your backup key to log into *one* account.

✓ **Check password manager health**

Audit weak or reused passwords.

✓ **Remove old devices**

Google / Apple / Microsoft all accumulate device listings.

✓ **Update your router**

Firmware updates = better protection.

This simple routine keeps your security constantly sharp.

Chapter Summary

You now possess the expert-level strategies used by cybersecurity professionals.

You've learned:

✓ **The Three-Key Rotation System**

✓ **Multi-browser WebAuthn protection**

✓ **The Device Trust Map**

✓ **How to centralize emergency access**

✓ **How to protect yourself offline**

✓ **How to secure forgotten high-risk accounts**

✓ **How to compartmentalize YubiKeys**

✓ **Workarounds for portless devices**

✓ **Perfect naming strategies**

✓ **Safe key replacement**

✓ **Quarterly expert audit techniques**

With this chapter complete, you are now capable of designing a **military-grade digital security system** for yourself, your business, and your entire family.

You are operating at a level few people ever reach.

Chapter 12 — Your Unhackable Life (Putting It All Together)

This is the final transformation. Everything you've learned — every key, every setting, every freeze, every backup plan — comes together here into one unified system. This is the blueprint of a truly unhackable life.

This chapter is your *summary, your completion, and your future roadmap.*

We'll walk through:

- The full security stack you've built
- The philosophy behind living securely
- How to maintain your system for life
- How to protect future accounts
- How to handle life changes (new devices, new banks, new jobs)
- A simple annual routine
- A final checklist you can print and keep
- A concluding message for the next chapter of your life

Let's bring everything together.

The Security Stack You Built (A Master Overview)

You now have a COMPLETE layered defense system, stronger than what most banks, corporations, and government agencies use internally.

Here's your finished structure — the **Unhackable Life Security Pyramid**:

Top Layer — Identity Shield

- Credit freezes (all bureaus)
- ChexSystems freeze
- LexisNexis freeze
- IRS IP PIN enabled
- SSA account secured
- Medicare.gov secured

Middle Layer — Account Armor

- YubiKeys on every critical account
- Password manager master password hardened
- Backup keys registered everywhere

- Browser/device audit complete
- SMS removed
- Old recovery methods purged

Base Layer — Home & Family Firewall

- Router secured
- IoT devices isolated
- Firewalla or equivalent network protection (if available)
- Family members secured
- Elderly parents protected
- Family emergency plan established

You didn't just plug holes.You built a full fortress.

The Three Laws of Living Unhackable

You don't need to memorize everything from this book.Just these three laws:

Law #1 — Never Trust SMS Verification

SMS is dead.SIM swaps, phishing, spoofing — it's all too easy.

You've replaced SMS with YubiKeys everywhere.Never go back.

Law #2 — Protect the Email, Protect the Kingdom

Your email is your "reset switch" for all accounts.

If your email is secured with a YubiKey and a strong password:

- Hackers can't reset your bank login
- They can't reset your Apple ID
- They can't reset your Amazon
- They can't access your password manager

The fortress begins with email.

Law #3 — Maintain Backups Like a Pilot

Pilots don't fly without redundant systems.

And neither should you.

You have:

- A primary YubiKey
- A backup YubiKey
- Possibly an emergency offsite key

- A documented recovery plan
- Redundancy = resilience.Resilience = security.

How to Add Future Accounts the Right Way

Whenever you create a new account — bank, email, app, website, anything — follow this simple three-step process:

Step 1 — Add it to your password manager

Generate a strong unique password.

Step 2 — Immediately enable the strongest available 2FA

Preferably:

Security Key (best)

TOTP app (second best)

Anything else (only if forced)

Step 3 — Register BOTH YubiKeys

Never register only one.

If the service allows only one?Create two accounts: one for the primary and one for the backup if needed(or monitor for future support).

How to Handle New Devices Securely

When you buy a new phone or computer:

1. Secure it BEFORE using it for anything sensitive

- Update system
- Update browser
- Install password manager
- Register the device in your accounts

2. Remove old devices from account dashboards

Do this at:

- Google
- Apple
- Microsoft
- Banks
- Password manager

3. Re-register YubiKeys if needed

Some apps or browsers require re-enrollment when switching devices.

Handling Life Changes (Divorce, Death, Moves, New Jobs)

Security plans must adapt.

Here's how:

Moving to a new home

- Update your safe location
- Update mailing address freezes
- Reconfirm account recovery information

Changing phone numbers

- Update all accounts
- Remove old number
- Rely on YubiKeys, not SMS

Divorce

- Change all passwords
- Audit all recovery emails
- Immediately revoke all devices you do not trust
- Replace both YubiKeys and re-register everywhere
- Update your emergency plan

Death of a spouse/family member

- Secure their accounts
- Freeze their credit
- Lock down their email
- Remove old authentication options
- Update your family emergency kit

New job or business venture

- Keep business YubiKeys separate
- Secure payroll portals
- Secure tax documents
- Secure business banking

- Life changes — your security must evolve with it.

The Two-Step Annual Security Routine

Perform this once per year.

It takes about 1 hour and keeps you invincible.

Step 1 — Run the Full Annual Audit

From Chapter 10:

- Check freezes
- Test both YubiKeys
- Update router firmware
- Remove old devices
- Audit password manager
- Check all financial accounts
- Update emergency kit

Step 2 — Update Your Family Plan

- New keys? Document them.
- New accounts? Secure them.
- Kids older now? Add teen protections.

- Elderly parents need more help? Add keys.
- Did you move? Update safe storage.

This keeps your system **living** and **current**.

The "Unhackable Mindset"

Technology isn't the whole story.Mindset matters.

Here are the five traits of an unhackable person:

1. Awareness Over Fear

Security isn't about paranoia — it's about preparation.

2. Consistency Over Complexity

Simple routines beat complicated systems.

3. Proactivity Over Passivity

You set your security BEFORE something happens.

4. Redundancy Over Trust

Backups are the foundation of digital safety.

5. Confidence Over Confusion

When you understand your system, you stop feeling overwhelmed.

You now have this mindset.

Your Final Unhackable Life Checklist (Print This)

Identity Protection

✓ Credit frozen (all bureaus)

✓ ChexSystems frozen

✓ LexisNexis frozen

✓ IRS IP PIN enabled

✓ SSA/Medicare secure

Account Protection

✓ Email secured with YubiKey

✓ Password manager secured

✓ Banks secured

✓ Investments secured

✓ Apple/Google/Microsoft secured

✓ Backup key registered everywhere

✓ SMS removed

Family Security

✓ Spouse protected

✓ Teens protected

✓ Elderly parents protected

✓ Emergency kit created

✓ Recovery plan documented

Home Security

✓ Router secured

✓ IoT isolated

✓ Firewall enabled

✓ Network segmented

Ongoing Maintenance

✓ Quarterly check

✓ Annual audit

✓ Update devices

✓ Review recovery methods

✓ Rotate keys if needed

You now possess a complete, lifelong system.

Final Thoughts: You Did Something Extraordinary

Most people know they should protect their accounts, but they never do.

Most people know passwords aren't enough, but they do nothing.

Most people fear hacks, but they never act.

You acted. You secured yourself. You secured your family. You built redundancy. You built resilience. You built a fortress.

And you built a system that will protect you for the rest of your life.

You've joined the very small group of people who are:

- Unphishable
- Unscammable
- Unspoofable
- Unbreakable
- And most importantly...
- **Unhackable.**

This is your system now. Your fortress. Your peace of mind.

You earned it.

▧ Appendix A — Quick Start Guides, Checklists & Templates

This appendix is designed for *fast action.*It gives readers the **shortest, simplest possible instructions** for each major task covered in the book.

Quick Start: Setting Up Your YubiKey (5 Steps)

Buy two YubiKeys (primary + backup).

Secure your email first

— Gmail/Outlook/iCloud.

Secure your password manager (Bitwarden, 1Password).

Secure your financial accounts (banks + brokerage).

Register your backup key everywhere at the same time.

Quick Setup Checklist (Print This)

✓ **Purchase**

- Two YubiKeys
- Fireproof safe
- Optional: safe deposit box

✓ **Primary Accounts Secured**

- Gmail / Outlook
- Apple ID / Google Account
- Password manager
- Bank
- Investments
- Social Security
- IRS account with IP PIN

✓ **Backup Ready**

- Backup key registered on all accounts
- Backup stored safely
- Recovery sheet printed

✓ **Cleanup Completed**

SMS disabled

- Old devices removed
- Old 2FA removed
- Security questions deleted

New Account Template

Whenever you create a new account, follow this template.

Account Name: ________________**Username:** ____________________**Password stored in PM:** Yes / No**Primary YubiKey registered:** Yes / No**Backup YubiKey registered:** Yes / No**Recovery options updated:** Yes / No

Emergency Recovery Sheet (Simplified)

Store this **printed** in your safe.

Primary YubiKey location: ____________________

Backup YubiKey location: _____________________

Emergency key location (optional): ___________

Password manager master password recovery instructions stored where?

Bank support numbers: _________________________

Credit freeze PINs stored where? _____________

Family Security Plan Checklist

Parents

✓ Emails secured

✓ Phones secured

✓ Password managers secured

✓ Banks locked with YubiKeys

Teens

✓ Email + phone secure

✓ Social media secure

✓ Gaming accounts secure

✓ Parent holds backup key

Elderly Parents

✓ Bank accounts secured

✓ SSA.gov secured

✓ Medicare.gov secured

✓ You hold their backup key

Annual Audit Checklist

Print and complete every year.

Identity

✓ Credit froze

✓ ChexSystems froze

✓ LexisNexis froze

✓ IRS IP PIN active

Accounts

✓ YubiKeys tested

✓ Backup tested

✓ Old devices removed

✓ Password manager audited

Home

✓ Router updated

✓ IoT isolated

✓ Firewall enabled

Travel Security Sheet

Bring

- Primary YubiKey
- Phone + charger
- Password manager access
- Offline recovery notes

Leave Home

- Backup key
- Emergency key
- Recovery sheets

Avoid

- Public PCs
- Hotel Wi-Fi logins
- USB charging ports without adapters

Family Emergency Instructions Sheet

Store in a fireproof safe.

If I Lose Access to My Accounts:

Retrieve backup YubiKey from:

Unlock password manager using:

Access banks using:

Contact these institutions immediately:

Bank fraud hotline: ____________________

Credit freeze PIN recovery: ___________

IRS support: ____________________________

SSA support: ____________________________

Notes for family/executor:

Elderly Parent Protection Worksheet

Parent Name: ____________________________**Primary YubiKey location:** _______________**Backup YubiKey held by:** __________________

Accounts secured:

Gmail / Outlook

Bank

Medicare

MyChart

Pharmacy portals

Additional Notes:

Recovery Drill Worksheet (Quarterly Test)

Every 3 months:

Primary key tested: Yes / No **Backup key tested:** Yes / No **Password manager emergency kit current:** Yes / No **Backup key location verified:** Yes / No **New accounts added to PM:** Yes / No **Device trust list cleaned:** Yes / No

Notes:

Device & Browser Audit Sheet

Devices You Use:

- Laptop 1
- Laptop 2
- Phone
- Tablet
- Work computer

Browsers You Use:

- Chrome
- Firefox
- Safari

- Edge

Old devices removed? Yes / No**Old browsers removed?** Yes / No

Annual Financial Security Checklist (Expanded)

Identity

- Credit freezes verified
- LexisNexis freeze
- ChexSystems freeze
- IRS IP PIN renewed

Financial

- Banks audited
- Brokerage accounts secured
- Retirement account security verified
- Fraud alerts configured

Digital

- YubiKeys tested
- Backup key tested
- Browsers updated
- Password audit complete

Home

- Router firmware updated
- Network segmentation reviewed
- IoT devices rechecked

Continue the Journey

If this book resonated with you, here's where to go next:

Network Essentials *(Recommended Next)*
A step-by-step guide to setting up a Firewalla firewall.

Firewalla: After Setup

Firewalla: After Setup focuses on the decisions that matter once your network is running: how to structure devices, reduce noise, contain risk, and keep security effective over time — without constant tweaking.

For readers interested in exploring Awareness,

Awareness *(Recommended Next)*
Noticing What's Already Here
Begin by noticing the voice inside your head and stepping out of automatic identification with it.

Still Noticing
Living with Awareness in Daily Life
Continue noticing how awareness shows up in real situations, habits, and patterns.

After Awareness
What Happens Next
Explore what unfolds over time as awareness becomes part of how you live.

All titles are part of the **Personal Security in a Digital World** *series.*

Bitwarden Essentials

A practical guide to securing and managing your passwords using Bitwarden, with step-by-step instructions for setup, daily use, and account recovery.

Guard Your Money

A clear, practical guide to protecting financial accounts using YubiKey hardware security, covering phishing, identity theft, and modern account takeover threats.

Network Security Essentials

A plain-language guide to securing a home network using Firewalla Gold Plus, focused on understanding security choices rather than just technical settings.

Firewalla: After Setup

Firewalla: After Setup focuses on the decisions that matter once your network is running: how to structure devices, reduce noise, contain risk, and keep security effective over time — without constant tweaking.

The Awareness Series

These books explore awareness as it is experienced — not as a concept, but as something noticed in real time.

Awareness

Noticing the Voice Inside Your Head
The starting point — recognizing the voice and stepping out of automatic identification with it.

Still Noticing

Living with Awareness in Daily Life
What happens after the initial shift — when awareness meets real situations, habits, and patterns.

After Awareness

What Happens Next

The continuation — living with awareness over time, including the parts that are often left out.

These books can be read in any order, but they follow a natural progression:

Awareness → Still Noticing → After Awareness

Also Available from Prairie Light Press

The **Awareness Series** explores the nature of thought, attention, and the sense of self—through direct observation, not theory.

Written in clear, simple language, these books are designed to be experienced, not analyzed.

Available worldwide in Kindle and paperback editions.

Visit:

Prairie Light Press
https://www.prairielightpress.com

Also Available from Prairie Light Press

The ***Personal Security in a Digital World*** series helps readers protect passwords, financial accounts, and home networks using practical, plain-language guidance.

Available worldwide in Kindle and paperback editions.

Visit:

Prairie Light Press

http://www.prairielightpress.com/

Prairie Light Dispatch
For more reflections on awareness, life, and technology,
visit *Prairie Light Dispatch* on Substack at

Prairie Light Dispatch

https://lgphil7.substack.com/

Continue Reading for an

Exclusive Prairie Light Press Reader Preview

Of

Network Security Essentials

A Guide to Securing Your Network with Firewalla Gold Plus

Continue Your Journey

You've taken an important step toward protecting your digital life by securing your passwords and your financial and other important accounts using a YubiKey..

But password and account security is only one piece of a larger picture.

We believe in a layered approach to security, adding one layer at a time. Other layers to address are Identity, and of course, what all of it travels through, your Home or Small Business Network.

Prairie Light Press publishes books on technology, security, financial protection, and personal awareness—all designed to help you make better decisions in an increasingly complex world.

The following pages contain a preview of another Prairie Light Press title.

Book Preview

Network Security Essentials

A Guide to Securing Your Network with Firewalla Gold Plus

Turn the page to enjoy an exclusive preview from Prairie Light Press.

Network Security Essentials

A Guide to Securing Your Network

with Firewalla Gold Plus

An independent, unofficial guide

L. Phillips

Helping readers move from the unknown to the known

Network Security Essentials
A Guide to Securing Your Network

English Edition

Third Edition

Disclaimer

The information in this book is provided for educational and informational purposes only. While every effort has been made to ensure accuracy, technology and security practices evolve over time.

The author makes no guarantees regarding the effectiveness of any tools, techniques, or strategies discussed and assumes no responsibility for errors, omissions, or outcomes resulting from the use of this information.

Readers are encouraged to evaluate their own circumstances and, where appropriate, consult qualified professionals before implementing security, financial, or technical decisions.

Non-Affiliation Notice: This book is an independent publication and is not affiliated with, endorsed by, or sponsored by any company or organization mentioned herein, including but not limited to Firewalla.

Contents of the Complete Book
Page numbers refer to the full edition.

Table of Contents

How I Came to Take Home Network Security Seriously

I didn't start thinking seriously about network security because I wanted to become an expert, or because I enjoyed tinkering with technology for its own sake. I started because, over time, I became uncomfortable with how much of my personal life flowed invisibly through my home network—and how little visibility or control I actually had over it.

Like most people, I relied for years on the equipment provided by my internet service provider. It worked well enough. Devices connected. Streaming played. Emails sent. On the surface, everything functioned as expected. But beneath that surface, I realized I had no meaningful way to answer simple questions: What devices were actually on my network? Where was my data going? Which connections were normal, and which weren't?

That discomfort grew as the number of connected devices in my home increased. Phones, laptops, smart TVs, cameras, streaming boxes, voice assistants—each added convenience, but also complexity. Each one introduced software written by someone else, communicating with servers I didn't control, in ways I couldn't easily see. I wasn't

paranoid, but I was increasingly aware that "working" wasn't the same as "secure."

I began looking for ways to gain visibility and control without turning my home into an IT project. I wasn't interested in enterprise firewalls, subscription-heavy security services, or tools that required constant attention. I wanted something that respected privacy, ran locally, and made the network understandable rather than opaque.

That search eventually led me to Firewalla.

What stood out wasn't just the feature list, but the philosophy behind it: local processing, clear visibility, and tools that assume the user wants to understand what's happening—not just be told that things are "safe." Over time, as I used Firewalla in my own network, I realized that many of the questions I had struggled to answer were the same questions others were asking as well.

This book grew out of that experience.

It's not written as a marketing guide or a replacement for official documentation. It's written as a practical companion—one that explains not just how to configure Firewalla, but why certain choices matter, how features fit together, and how to think about your home network as a system worth understanding and maintaining.

If you've ever felt that your network works, but you don't really know *how* or *why*, you're in the right place.

Introduction

Your home network is more than just a way to get online. It's the infrastructure that connects everything in your digital life—computers, phones, smart speakers, security cameras, thermostats, game consoles, streaming devices. Everything.

And like any infrastructure, it needs management, security, and maintenance. That's where Firewalla comes in.

This book is your complete guide to the Firewalla Gold Plus—a powerful network security device that gives you professional-grade protection and control over your home network. Whether you're setting up Firewalla for the first time or looking to master its advanced features, you'll find practical, actionable information here.

About Firewalla

Firewalla is a hardware firewall and network security device. It sits between your modem and your network, protecting everything behind it while giving you unprecedented visibility and control.

Think of Firewalla as combining two core roles: **Protection & Privacy** and **Control & Management**.

Protection & Privacy

- **Firewall:** Blocks unwanted connections and intrusion attempts
- **Content filtering:** Blocks ads, trackers, malware, and inappropriate content
- **VPN server:** Lets you securely connect to your network from anywhere
- **VPN client:** Routes traffic through privacy services
- **Network monitoring:** Shows exactly what's happening on your network

Control & Management

- **Parental controls:** Manages when and what kids can access
- **Network management:** Creates separate networks for different purposes

Why Do You Need It?

Modern home networks face challenges that didn't exist a decade ago. Consider what's changed:

More Devices, More Vulnerabilities

The average home now has 25+ connected devices. Each one is a potential entry point for attackers. Your router's basic firewall wasn't designed for this scale or complexity.

Privacy Is Under Attack

Companies track your browsing across websites. Advertisers build detailed profiles about you and your family. Your ISP can see and log every site you visit. Smart devices send data about your habits back to their manufacturers.

Kids Need Protection

Children have unprecedented access to the internet through phones, tablets, and computers. Keeping them safe requires more than just hoping they make good choices—it needs technical guardrails.

IoT Devices Are Insecure

Smart speakers, cameras, door locks, and thermostats are notoriously poorly secured. Many have known vulnerabilities. Some send data you didn't know they were collecting. They need to be isolated from your important devices.

Remote Access Needs Security

Working from home, accessing your NAS while traveling, or checking security cameras remotely all require secure connections. Your router's basic features aren't enough.

You Want Control

Your network, your rules. You should decide what's allowed, when it's allowed, and who can do what. Consumer routers offer minimal control. Firewalla gives you complete authority over your network.

What Makes Firewalla Gold Plus Special?

Firewalla makes several models. The Gold Plus (often called Gold) is the sweet spot for most users—powerful enough for demanding networks but not overkill for typical homes.

Key Specifications

- Quad-core 1.5 GHz processor: Handles deep packet inspection at full gigabit speeds
- 4 GB RAM: Enough for extensive rule sets and monitoring
- 6 Gigabit Ethernet ports: 1 WAN + 4 LAN + 1 additional multi-purpose port
- Up to 1 Gbps throughput: Won't bottleneck your internet connection
- Up to 5 VLANs: Create virtually separated networks
- Dual-WAN support: Use two internet connections for redundancy or combined bandwidth
- Silent operation: Fanless design, no noise
- Compact size: Fits anywhere, no rack required

What You Can Do With It

Security

Block malware, phishing, and intrusion attempts automatically
See every connection every device makes
Isolate vulnerable IoT devices
Get alerts when suspicious activity occurs
Block ads and trackers network-wide

Privacy

Run your own VPN server for secure remote access
Route traffic through commercial VPN services
Block tracking and data collection
Control what information leaves your network

Parental Controls

Filter content by category (adult, violence, gambling, etc.)
Set time limits on internet usage
See what sites kids are visiting
Block specific apps or games
Create schedules that adapt to school days vs weekends

Network Management

Create separate networks (main, guest, IoT, work)
See bandwidth usage by device
Prioritize important traffic (video calls over downloads)
Set bandwidth limits
Manage two internet connections

Who This Book Is For

This book is written for people who:

Just bought a Firewalla Gold Plus and want to set it up properly

- Have Firewalla running but aren't using most of its features
- Want to understand what Firewalla is doing and why
- Need to solve specific problems (slow internet, security concerns, parental controls)
- Want to master advanced features like VLANs and policy-based routing

You don't need to be a network engineer. Technical concepts are explained in plain language with real-world examples. When technical terms are necessary, they're defined clearly.

That said, this isn't a dumbed-down guide. We cover sophisticated features and assume you want to understand how things actually work, not just click buttons. If you want to learn, you'll find detailed explanations. If you just want to get something done, you'll find step-by-step instructions.

What This Book Covers

The book is organized to work both as a learning path and as a reference:

Chapters 2-3: Getting Started

Installation, initial configuration, and basic operation. Get Firewalla protecting your network quickly.

Chapters 4-7: Core Features

Dashboard navigation, device management, security features, and parental controls. The features you'll use daily.

Chapters 8-11: Advanced Features

VPN server and client, advanced networking, troubleshooting, and performance monitoring. Power user territory.

Chapters 12-15: Expert Topics

Advanced rules, security deep-dive, automation, and maintenance. For users who want complete mastery.

Appendices

Quick reference guides, troubleshooting checklist, and glossary.

How to Use This Book

If You're Just Getting Started

Read Chapters 2-7 in order. They build on each other and will take you from unboxing to confident daily use. Don't skip ahead—later chapters assume you understand earlier concepts.

If You Have Specific Goals

Use the table of contents to find relevant chapters. Want to set up VPN? Chapter 8. Need to create separate networks? Chapter 9. Troubleshooting issues? Chapter 10. Want to optimize performance? Chapter 11.

If You're an Experienced User

You can probably skim Chapters 2-7 and focus on Chapters 8-15. But don't assume you know everything in the early chapters—Firewalla has some non-obvious features even experienced users miss.

As a Reference

Keep this book handy. When you encounter a feature or setting you don't understand, look it up. The index and table of contents make it easy to find information quickly.

Conventions Used in This Book

Navigation Paths

When instructions say to tap or click through menus, they're written like this: Settings -> System -> Updates. This means tap Settings, then System, then Updates.

Important Notes

Key information is called out in context. Pay attention to paragraphs that start with words like Important, Note, or Warning.

Screenshots

The book includes screenshots showing what you should see in the app. Your screen might look slightly different depending on your Firewalla model, app version, or network configuration, but the basic layout will be the same.

Example Scenarios

Throughout the book, you'll find example scenarios showing how to use features in real situations. These aren't hypothetical—they're based on actual use cases from real Firewalla users.

What You Need

Hardware

- Firewalla Gold Plus
- Internet connection (cable, fiber, DSL, etc.)
- Modem or ISP-provided gateway
- Smartphone or tablet for initial setup (iOS or Android)
- Ethernet cables

Optional But Recommended

- Managed network switch if you plan to use VLANs
- Separate Wi-Fi access point or mesh system (Firewalla doesn't include Wi-Fi)
- Computer for accessing web interface (some features are web-only)
- Backup internet connection if you're setting up dual-WAN

Knowledge

No networking expertise required, but basic computer skills help. You should be comfortable installing apps on your phone, connecting devices with Ethernet cables, following step-by-step instructions, and using a web browser.

Everything else you need to know is explained in the book.

Getting Help

This book covers most situations, but you might still have questions. Here's where to find help:

Firewalla Support

- Help center: help.firewalla.com - Searchable knowledge base
- Community forum: Discussions with other users and Firewalla staff
- Email support: help@firewalla.com
- In-app support: Tap the question mark icon in the app

This Book

- Index: Find specific topics quickly
- Troubleshooting appendix: Common problems and solutions
- Glossary: Definitions of technical terms

A Note About Versions

Firewalla releases updates regularly. The screenshots and specific menu locations in this book are accurate as of December 2024. If your app looks slightly different, that's normal—Firewalla improves the interface over time.

The core concepts and features remain stable. Even if a button moves or a screen is redesigned, the underlying functionality works the same way. Focus on understanding what features do, not just where to click.

Privacy and Data Collection

Firewalla takes privacy seriously. Understanding what data it collects and where it goes matters.

Local Processing

All security features, rule enforcement, and monitoring happen on your Firewalla box. Your network traffic doesn't route through Firewalla's cloud servers. They can't see what you're doing because the data never reaches them.

What Firewalla Cloud Receives

- Device names and groups (for multi-device app sync)
- Rule configurations (so they sync across devices)
- Anonymous usage statistics (what features are used, not what traffic flows through)
- Alarm summaries for notifications (but not full traffic logs)

What Firewalla Never Receives

- Your actual internet traffic content
- Websites you visit
- Files you download
- Messages or communications
- Video streams or media content

You control your data. If you prefer, you can disable cloud sync entirely and manage everything locally, though you'll lose convenient features like remote access to the app and push notifications.

Ready to Begin

Network security isn't just for IT professionals anymore. Your home network deserves the same protection businesses get. Firewalla brings enterprise-grade security to regular people, with an interface that makes sense and features you can actually use.

This book will teach you to use Firewalla effectively. You'll understand not just what to click, but why you're clicking it. You'll know how to diagnose problems, optimize performance, and configure advanced features with confidence.

By the time you finish, you'll have a secure, well-managed network that protects your family, respects your privacy, and works the way you want it to.

Ready? The next chapter covers getting Firewalla installed and configured.

Chapter 1: Meet Your Firewalla Gold Plus

Before we dive into installation and configuration, let's get acquainted with what you've purchased. The Firewalla Gold Plus isn't just another router or security appliance—it's a complete network security platform that happens to fit in the palm of your hand.

Understanding what your Firewalla Gold Plus can do, and equally important, understanding its design philosophy, will help you make the most of its capabilities. This chapter walks you through the hardware, the core features, and the thinking behind why it works the way it does.

The Hardware

Physical Design

The Firewalla Gold Plus is compact—roughly the size of a small hardcover book. The metal chassis serves dual purposes: it protects the internal components and acts as a heat sink for passive cooling. There's no fan, which means no noise and one less component to fail.

The fanless design isn't just about silence. Fans collect dust, wear out bearings, and become points of failure. A passively cooled system that's properly designed will outlast its actively cooled counterparts. The chassis gets warm during operation—that's normal and by design. It's dissipating heat effectively without requiring moving parts.

The unit weighs enough to feel substantial but not so much that you can't mount it on a wall. Speaking of which, it comes with mounting hardware if you want to keep it out of the way. Most people either mount it near their networking equipment or simply set it on a shelf where it has good ventilation.

Ports and Connections

All the action happens on the back panel:

- **Four 2.5 Gigabit Ethernet ports: These are your network connections. One typically connects to your internet (WAN), and the others connect to your local network (LAN). But Firewalla is flexible—you can configure these ports in various ways depending on your needs.** They're color-coded and numbered, which helps during setup.
- **Two USB 3.0 ports:** One is occupied by a red security dongle (don't remove this—it's tied to your device). The other can be used for the optional Wi-Fi adapter or future expansions.
- **HDMI port:** This provides console access if you ever need to troubleshoot at a low level. Most users will never touch this.
- **Serial console port:** Another troubleshooting interface that you'll likely never need. It's there for advanced scenarios.
- **Power input:** Standard DC power input. The included power adapter is compact and efficient, drawing less than 15 watts on average—about the same as an LED light bulb.

The front panel has a power button (primarily for shutdown) and a reset button. The reset button should only be used as a last resort when something goes wrong. The power button is mainly for graceful shutdowns—the system boots automatically when power is applied.

The 2.5 Gigabit Advantage

Most home networking equipment uses Gigabit Ethernet (1 Gbps). The Gold Plus uses 2.5 Gigabit (2.5 Gbps) ports. This might seem like overkill if your internet connection is "only" 1 Gbps, but there's method to this apparent madness.

First, internet speeds are increasing. Multi-gigabit fiber is becoming more common, and cable companies are pushing speeds beyond 1 Gbps. The Gold Plus is ready for this without requiring replacement.

Second, and more immediately relevant: security processing has overhead. When Firewalla examines every packet flowing through your network—checking for threats, applying rules, logging activity—that takes processing power. With 1 Gbps ports, you might see your effective throughput drop to 700-800 Mbps under heavy security processing. With 2.5 Gbps ports, you maintain full gigabit speeds even with comprehensive security enabled.

Third, your internal network traffic benefits. Backing up a computer to a NAS, streaming high-bitrate video from a local server, or transferring large files between devices—these activities happen at LAN speeds, not internet speeds. The faster ports mean these local transfers complete faster.

The Gold Plus is rated for up to 5 Gbps of total packet processing throughput. This means it can handle multiple 2.5 Gbps streams simultaneously or process data at line rate with security features enabled.

Inside the Box

The Gold Plus is built around an Intel J4125 processor—a quad-core chip designed for efficiency and reliability. It has 4GB of RAM and runs a custom Linux distribution that's been optimized for network security tasks.

This is important because unlike consumer routers that use generic firmware, Firewalla's software is purpose-built. Every component of the system is designed to work together: the hardware acceleration for encryption, the network processing, the storage management, and the security analysis.

The system boots from eMMC flash storage—solid-state memory that's faster and more reliable than SD cards or spinning hard drives. This contributes to the quick boot times (the system is typically ready in under a minute) and the system's overall responsiveness.

Core Capabilities

The hardware is the foundation, but the software is where Firewalla really shines. Let's walk through what it actually does for you.

Network Visibility

The first thing Firewalla does is show you what's happening on your network. Not in the abstract "there's traffic" sense, but specifically: what device is connecting to what service, how much bandwidth it's using, when it's active, and what kind of data is flowing.

Every device on your network gets identified. Firewalla recognizes the manufacturer, device type, and in many cases, the specific model. Your iPhone shows up as an iPhone, not just as "Unknown Device." Your smart TV is labeled as a TV. Your printer is clearly marked as a printer.

For each device, you can see:

- **What domains and services it connects to:** Is your smart TV talking to Netflix, or is it also sending data to advertising networks?
- **Bandwidth usage over time:** Which devices are consuming the most data, and when?
- **Connection patterns:** When is the device most active? Are there unusual connection spikes?
- **Security alerts:** Any blocked threats or suspicious activity associated with this device.

This visibility isn't about surveillance—it's about understanding. When something goes wrong (your internet seems slow, a device isn't connecting properly, you're worried about security), you have the data to figure out what's actually happening rather than guessing.

Active Protection

Firewalla doesn't just observe—it protects. The system includes several layers of active defense that work automatically once enabled:

Intrusion Detection and Prevention (IDS/IPS)

The system watches for known attack patterns and malicious behavior. When it detects something suspicious—port scanning, exploit attempts, command-and-control traffic—it can alert you or block it automatically.

This happens at network speed. The IDS/IPS engine examines traffic in real-time, comparing it against a database of threat signatures that's updated regularly. When you enable Active Protect, you're not just blocking known malware sites—you're stopping exploit attempts, preventing unauthorized access, and catching threats before they reach your devices.

Ad and Tracker Blocking

Firewalla can block ads and trackers at the network level. This is different from browser ad blockers—it works for every device and every app on your network. Your smart TV's ads disappear. Your kids' tablets stop showing inappropriate advertising. Mobile apps that are riddled with ads become usable.

The ad blocking uses curated blocklists that identify advertising and tracking domains. When a device tries to connect to these domains, Firewalla simply refuses the connection. To the app or website, it looks like the ad server is unavailable. The content loads, minus the ads.

You can customize this extensively. Use aggressive blocking to remove nearly all ads and trackers, or use lighter filtering that only blocks the most intrusive content. You can also whitelist specific sites if blocking causes problems.

Malware and Phishing Protection

The system maintains blocklists of known malware distribution sites, phishing domains, and command-and-control servers. These are updated continuously. When any device on your network tries to connect to a blocked domain, the connection is refused and you receive an alert.

This protection works even if the device itself is compromised. A infected computer trying to "phone home" to its controllers will be blocked. A user clicking a phishing link will be stopped before reaching the fake site. This is your network-level immune system.

Behavioral Analysis

Beyond signature-based detection, Firewalla watches for unusual behavior. A device that suddenly starts uploading massive amounts of data, a new device appearing on your network without your knowledge, connection patterns that don't match normal usage—these trigger alerts.

The system learns what's normal for your network over time. This means it gets better at distinguishing between legitimate activity and potential problems. It's not about paranoid false alarms—it's about surfacing genuinely unusual events that deserve your attention.

Network Control

Visibility and protection are important, but control is where you shape your network to work the way you want:

Rules and Policies

You can create rules that control what happens on your network. Block a specific website. Limit bandwidth for a device or application. Prevent certain devices from communicating with each other. Route traffic through a VPN. The possibilities are extensive.

Rules can be simple ("Block Facebook on my kids' devices") or sophisticated ("Route all traffic from my work laptop through my company VPN, except local network traffic, but only during business hours"). The app provides templates for common scenarios, so you don't need to think like a network engineer to create useful policies.

Family Protect Controls

Firewalla includes robust parental control features. You can filter content by category (block adult content, gambling, social media, gaming), set usage schedules (internet access only during certain hours), and pause the internet for specific devices or users.

The "Social Hour" feature is particularly clever—it blocks all social media for one-hour increments, making it easy to enforce screen-free family time without completely cutting off internet access. Kids can still do homework that requires web access; they just can't scroll TikTok during dinner.

Safe Search enforcement ensures that search engines return filtered results, even if the child tries to disable safe search. And all of this works regardless of what device they're using or whether they've installed blocking software—it's enforced at the network level.

Network Segmentation

One of the Gold Plus's most powerful features is the ability to create separate network segments. Think of these as virtual walls within your network.

You might create a guest network that has internet access but can't see or connect to your personal devices. Or an IoT network for smart home devices that's isolated from your computers and phones. Or a kids' network with strict filtering and time limits while your main network remains unrestricted.

Each segment can have its own rules, policies, and security settings. Devices on one segment can't see devices on another unless you explicitly allow it. This is how enterprises protect their networks, and now you can do the same at home.

Bandwidth Management

Smart Queue is Firewalla's traffic prioritization feature. It ensures that your video calls don't lag when someone else is downloading a large file. Gaming traffic gets priority when needed. Video streaming is managed to prevent buffering without hogging all the bandwidth.

You can also set hard limits: this device gets no more than X Mbps, or this activity type gets throttled during certain hours. It's your bandwidth—you decide how it's allocated.

VPN Capabilities

The Gold Plus includes comprehensive VPN support in both directions:

VPN Server

When you're away from home, you can connect back to your home network securely. This means:

- Access to your home network resources (files, printers, security cameras) from anywhere
- Your internet traffic appears to come from home, which can be useful for accessing geo-restricted content or avoiding suspicious public Wi-Fi networks
- All the security and filtering you have at home extends to your devices wherever you are

The system supports both OpenVPN and WireGuard protocols. WireGuard is newer, faster, and particularly good for mobile devices. OpenVPN is more established and works through more types of networks. You can enable both simultaneously.

Setting up VPN access is remarkably simple—the app generates configuration profiles that you can install on your devices with a few taps. No manual configuration of IP addresses or certificates required.

VPN Client

Firewalla can also act as a VPN client, connecting your entire network (or specific devices) through a commercial VPN service. This is useful if you want to:

- Route all your home traffic through a VPN for privacy

- Access content as if you're in a different country
- Protect devices that can't run VPN software themselves (smart TVs, game consoles)

The advantage of doing VPN at the router level is that it covers every device automatically. You don't need to configure VPN on each computer, phone, and tablet. Change VPN providers or servers? Update it once in Firewalla and all your devices get the new settings.

You can even get selective: route only certain devices through the VPN, or only certain types of traffic. Your work laptop goes through your company VPN while everything else uses your regular internet connection. Your smart TV goes through a VPN for streaming while your gaming console uses the direct connection for lower latency.

Router Mode vs. Simple Mode

The Firewalla Gold Plus can operate in different modes, and understanding these modes will help you set it up correctly for your situation.

Simple Mode (DHCP Mode)

In Simple Mode, Firewalla sits alongside your existing router. Your router continues to handle routing and DHCP (assigning IP addresses to devices). Firewalla monitors all the traffic and applies its security features, but it doesn't replace your router.

This mode is ideal when:

- You rent your router from your ISP and can't easily replace it

- You have a mesh network system that you want to keep using
- You want to add security without changing your current network setup
- You're not comfortable with advanced networking changes

The installation is straightforward: plug Firewalla into one of your router's LAN ports and connect your devices to Firewalla's ports. The system automatically configures itself.

Simple Mode gives you all of Firewalla's security and monitoring features. The main limitation is that you can't take full advantage of network segmentation or advanced routing features—your existing router is still handling those functions.

Router Mode

In Router Mode, Firewalla becomes your router. It connects directly to your modem and handles all routing, DHCP, and network management duties. Your existing router either gets removed or is put into "bridge mode" (effectively turning it into just a Wi-Fi access point).

This mode unlocks the full capabilities of the Gold Plus:

- Full network segmentation with isolated VLANs
- Multi-WAN support (multiple internet connections, load balancing, and failover)
- Advanced routing policies
- Complete control over DHCP and DNS settings

- Better performance (no double-NAT or routing overhead)

Router Mode is the recommended configuration if you own your equipment and are comfortable making networking changes. It's not particularly difficult—the app walks you through it—but it does require connecting to your modem directly and potentially reconfiguring your Wi-Fi access points.

One important note: the Gold Plus doesn't have built-in Wi-Fi. In Router Mode, you'll need separate Wi-Fi access points or routers running in access point mode. This might sound like a limitation, but it's actually an advantage—you can use whichever Wi-Fi solution works best for your space, and you can upgrade your Wi-Fi independently from your security and routing.

Bridge Mode

Bridge Mode is a specialized configuration where Firewalla sits transparently between your network segments. It's used in specific scenarios where you need to monitor traffic without changing IP addresses or network structure—typically for compatibility with complex existing setups.

Most users won't need Bridge Mode. It's mentioned here for completeness, but Simple Mode or Router Mode will handle the vast majority of home and small office setups.

What You Can't Do (And Why That's OK)

No product does everything, and Firewalla makes specific design choices that mean certain things aren't possible or aren't prioritized. Understanding these limitations helps set appropriate expectations.

No Built-in Wi-Fi

The Gold Plus doesn't include Wi-Fi. This is intentional—Wi-Fi access points and security appliances are different jobs that require different hardware. By separating them, you get better performance for both functions and the flexibility to choose the Wi-Fi solution that works for your space.

You can add a Wi-Fi USB adapter for specific use cases (like creating a temporary network or using a phone hotspot as backup internet), but for your main Wi-Fi, you'll use separate access points.

Not a Next-Gen Firewall for Enterprises

While the Gold Plus is powerful, it's designed for homes and small offices, not enterprise deployments. It doesn't have features like integration with Active Directory, sophisticated compliance reporting, or the redundancy and failover capabilities that large organizations require.

For a home or small business, this is perfectly appropriate. You get professional-grade security without paying for enterprise features you don't need.

No Subscription Required (But No Subscription Available Either)

Firewalla doesn't charge monthly or annual fees. You buy the hardware, and all features and updates are included. This is great for cost predictability, but it means certain service-based features aren't available.

For example, you can't pay for Firewalla to provide 24/7 monitoring and incident response. You're operating your own security—Firewalla gives you the tools, but you're the one using them. For most people, this trade-off (no recurring costs, but you're responsible for responding to alerts) is acceptable.

The Mobile App Philosophy

One of Firewalla's defining characteristics is that it's managed entirely through a mobile app. There's a web interface (currently in beta), but the app is the primary interface by design.

This might seem unusual if you're accustomed to configuring network equipment through web browsers. But consider: when was the last time you wanted to tweak your network security while sitting at a desk? Network security isn't something you configure once and forget—it's something you check from the couch, adjust when you see an alert on your phone, and modify when your kids ask why they can't access a site.

The app design reflects this usage pattern. It's information-dense but still clean. It provides quick access to common tasks (block this device, pause the internet, check bandwidth usage) while keeping advanced features available but out of the way.

Notifications appear where notifications belong—on your phone's lock screen. You don't need to remember to check a dashboard; alerts come to you. See something suspicious at 2 AM? Address it from your phone without getting out of bed.

Multiple people can have the app connected to the same Firewalla box. This is useful for families where parents might want to manage controls separately, or small businesses where multiple people share administrative duties.

Updates and Improvement

Firewalla's software is under continuous development. Updates are frequent—typically every few weeks—and they include both security updates and new features.

Updates happen automatically unless you disable this (not recommended). The system downloads updates in the background and applies them during low-traffic periods. You'll get a notification that an update was installed, but there's typically no disruption to your network.

This matters because the threat landscape changes constantly. New vulnerabilities are discovered, new attack patterns emerge, and new types of malicious behavior develop. Firewalla's update mechanism means you benefit from these improvements without having to do anything.

The company also maintains an active community forum where users discuss configurations, share tips, and request features. Many of the features added over the years came from user suggestions. This isn't abandoned-after-purchase hardware—it's an actively supported and improving platform.

Knowing Your Equipment

By now you should have a solid understanding of what the Firewalla Gold Plus is: a network security appliance designed for homes and small businesses that's powerful enough to provide professional-grade protection but accessible enough that you don't need to be a network engineer to use it effectively.

You know the hardware—four 2.5 Gbps ports, fanless cooling, efficient power consumption. You understand the core capabilities—visibility, protection, control, and VPN. You've learned about the different operating modes and when to use each. And you understand the design philosophy: mobile-first interface, continuous updates, and features that prioritize practical protection over theoretical completeness.

In the next chapter, we'll move from theory to practice and get your Firewalla Gold Plus installed and running on your network.

How I Came to Take Home Network Security Seriously

I didn't start thinking seriously about network security because I wanted to become an expert, or because I enjoyed tinkering with technology for its own sake. I started because, over time, I became uncomfortable with how much of my personal life flowed invisibly through my home network—and how little visibility or control I actually had over it.

Like most people, I relied for years on the equipment provided by my internet service provider. It worked well enough. Devices connected. Streaming played. Emails sent. On the surface, everything functioned as expected. But beneath that surface, I realized I had no meaningful way to answer simple questions: What devices were actually on my network? Where was my data going? Which connections were normal, and which weren't?

That discomfort grew as the number of connected devices in my home increased. Phones, laptops, smart TVs, cameras, streaming boxes, voice assistants—each added convenience, but also complexity. Each one introduced software written by someone else, communicating with servers I didn't control, in ways I couldn't easily see. I wasn't paranoid, but I was increasingly aware that "working" wasn't the same as "secure."

I began looking for ways to gain visibility and control without turning my home into an IT project. I wasn't interested in enterprise firewalls, subscription-heavy security services, or tools that required constant attention. I wanted something that respected privacy, ran locally, and made the network understandable rather than opaque.

That search eventually led me to Firewalla.

What stood out wasn't just the feature list, but the philosophy behind it: local processing, clear visibility, and tools that assume the user wants to understand what's happening—not just be told that things are "safe." Over time, as I used Firewalla in my own network, I realized that many of the questions I had struggled to answer were the same questions others were asking as well.

This book grew out of that experience.

It's not written as a marketing guide or a replacement for official documentation. It's written as a practical companion—one that explains not just how to configure Firewalla, but why certain choices matter, how features fit together, and how to think about your home network as a system worth understanding and maintaining.

If you've ever felt that your network works, but you don't really know *how* or *why*, you're in the right place.

Watch for more Prairie Light Press Reader Previews

www.ingramcontent.com/pod-product-compliance
Lightning Source LLC
LaVergne TN
LVHW091530200926
848483LV00002B/345